P9-DDO-474

THE
REFERENCE
SHELF

WOMEN'S ISSUES

Edited by ROBIN BROWN

THE REFERENCE SHELF

Volume 65 Number 5

The H. W. WILSON COMPANY

New York   1993

THE REFERENCE SHELF

The books in this series contain reprints of articles, excerpts from books, and addresses on current issues and social trends in the United States and other countries. There are six separately bound numbers in each volume, all of which are generally published in the same calendar year. One number is a collection of recent speeches; each of the others is devoted to a single subject and gives background information and discussion from various points of view, concluding with a comprehensive bibliography that contains books and pamphlets and abstracts of additional articles on the subject. Books in the series may be purchased individually or on subscription.

Library of Congress Cataloging-in-Publication Data

Women's issues / edited by Robin Brown.
    p.   cm.
    ISBN 0-8242-0844-7
    1. Women—United States—Social conditions. 2. Sex discrimination against women—United States. 3. Women—Employment—United States.
I. Brown, Robin, 1961– .
  HQ1421.W658 1993
  305.42'0973—dc20   93-4940
                                                   CIP

Cover: University of Oklahoma law professor Anita Hill is sworn in prior to testifying before the Senate Judiciary Committee on Capitol Hill.
Photo: AP/Wide World Photos

Printed in the United States of America

CONTENTS

III. WORK AND THE FAMILY

IV. THE NEW POLITICS

PREFACE

In October of 1991, Professor Anita Hill traveled to Washington to testify before the Senate Judiciary Committee regarding the nomination of Judge Clarence Thomas to the Supreme Court. She went to Washington to answer questions about her charge that Judge Thomas had persistently sexually harassed her ten years earlier, while he was her supervisor at the Equal Employment Opportunity Commission. National television broadcast her graphic testimony, in which she described these allegations in great detail. The Senate Judiciary Committee responded by trying to destroy her credibility and thereby casting doubts on her character and mental stability. Fourteen white middle-aged men faced a poised, professional African-American woman, and seemed incapable of imagining that she might be telling the truth. The mismanagement of Professor Hill's allegations and her treatment during the hearings angered many women. In effect, women were given a new symbol of the fact that they had not yet achieved equality in American society.

The Thomas-Hill hearings brought the subject of sexual harassment into the open. Women who had experienced it discovered that they were not alone, and men became very concerned about the level of social interaction that is appropriate in the workplace. What is sexual harassment? What is the difference between legal and illegal behavior? *Working Woman Magazine*'s June, 1992 survey of its readers reported that 60% of the people who returned the survey had experienced sexual harassment. In September of 1991, twenty-six women (including some naval officers) reported being manhandled by a large group of naval aviators at the Tailhook Association annual convention. It became clear that sexual harassment is not an isolated problem.

The publicity surrounding Tailhook and Anita Hill's testimony stimulated an examination of the status of women in the workplace. This volume focuses on some of the factors that make it difficult for women to achieve equality. The fault is not, as it was a generation ago, with unequal laws. Fear of legal action is but a short-term motivation that only touches on surface behavior. Laws may motivate managers to examine whether they are promoting a sufficiently diverse group of workers, but only mutual respect will get people to treat each other as equals. American society is a culture in conflict, in the midst of an unfinished evolution in gender roles. In previously male-dominated professions, this is a social change that may take a generation or more.

The first section in this volume illustrates both the opportunities and the struggles that women face as they enter into male-dominated fields. Why have women progressed so slowly? What are companies doing to encourage diversity in hiring and promotion? What legal recourse is available to a woman who has suffered discrimination? Are women happy in the workplace?

The second section examines the subject of sexual harassment and the Thomas-Hill hearings in greater detail. What is sexual harassment? What effect will the heightened awareness of sexual harassment have on a woman's status as a candidate for a position?

The third section examines the impact of family issues on the women's pursuit of equality in the workplace. In most cases, a woman who works outside the home still performs most of the cleaning, cooking and child-care. Can we come up with a more balanced structure that will benefit not only well-off, professional families, but also families that need affordable, reliable child-care in order to get off government assistance? To what extent should local and federal government get involved?

The fourth section of this compilation is a description of the 1992 presidential campaign and the issues it raised. The year 1992 was, more than anything else, a political year. Anger over Anita Hill's treatment by the U.S. Senate propelled a record number of women into political races. Women's political action committees (PACs), a key source of campaign funding, raised a record amount of money. In the presidential campaign, although the conservative wing of the Republican party laid claim to "family values", it seemed to be out of touch with what the American "family" has become. Against the symbolism of the Thomas-Hill hearings, the choice seemed to be between patriarchy, represented by George and Barbara Bush, and a new generation of equal partners, represented by Bill and Hillary Clinton.

All the topics in this volume are interrelated and the reader is urged to consider the selections in each section, rather than limiting their reading to the section that seems most relevant. Employment discrimination cannot, for example, be considered without examining the subtopics of harassment and family responsibilities because both problems limit a woman's ability to advance in her career. The final section is a vital reflection of our attitudes toward the sexes. Will we finally be equal when we have truly representative government?

The editor wishes to thank the authors and the publishers who kindly granted permission to reprint the material in this collection.

ROBIN BROWN

July 1993

I. WOMEN IN THE WORKPLACE

EDITOR'S INTRODUCTION

The women's movement of the 1960s and the early 1970s has deep roots in the struggle for equality between men and women in the workplace. Women's movement activists hoped that women would gain equality once they were protected against sexual discrimination in the workplace and assured of equal pay for their labor. The Equal Pay Act of 1961, though it was restricted in the types of jobs it covered, was the first breakthrough in federal legislation. In 1965, the feminist lobby successfully pushed for the addition of a prohibition against sexual discrimination to Title VII of the Civil Rights Act of 1964. Title VII thus eliminated many of the state protective labor laws that had kept women out of entire groups of occupations. The 1964 Civil Rights Act also authorized the creation of the Equal Employment Opportunity Commission (EEOC) to investigate claims of discrimination. In one of its earliest cases, championed by the feminist movement, the Commission, in 1968, banned airlines from firing stewardesses as "overage" at 32.

In the 25 years since that ruling, women have made progress in the range of occupations open to them. Unfortunately, many women still face hostile work environments in which they can be fired after requesting maternity leave, and a wage-gap that leaves women making just over 70 cents for every dollar a man makes. The first two articles in this section illustrate this mix of opportunity and discrimination. "When Will Women Get to the Top?" profile some women who are pioneers in the top ranks of corporate management. They are there, but widespread success for those behind them will probably take another generation. Senior managers are still much more likely to promote someone in their own image, thereby harming the chances of career advancement for both women and minorities. "Creating Change by Committee" is the story of the founding of the Female Employment Initiative, an organization that works to boost women's presence on construction sites in Chicago.

Unfortunately, the presence of women as equals in the work-place is not always welcome. "The Wage War Against Women" provides a summary of recent legal advances that now make it easier for victims of sexual discrimination to collect damages.

How many of the adjustments that are necessary to achieve equality should be accomplished by government mandate? In "Working Women's Staunchest Allies: Supply and Demand," Gary Becker, an economist at the University of Chicago, claims that the United States is getting much closer to achieving equal-pay for equal-work, regardless of gender or family situations, because of the law of supply and demand and civil rights legislation. There-fore, he argues, legislation for child-care leave is inefficient, un-just and unnecessary.

WHEN WILL WOMEN GET TO THE TOP?[1]

Talk for a while with any woman who has worked her way to the top of a sizable U.S. corporation. You'll get a strong sense that she feels a bit like *Apollo 14* astronaut Alan Shepard when he improvised a six iron out of a piece of lunar equipment and, one-handed in his cumbersome space suit, whacked a golf ball that flickered eerily across the airless surface of the moon. Exhila-rated, isolated, keenly aware of the world's attention ("*Houston, can you see me now?*"), female high executives are eager to colonize this unaccustomed terrain with more of their own. But like astro-nauts, they know too much about the rigors of the journey to believe that it can happen by next Wednesday, or even by next year. Says Carol Bartz, 44, recently named chairman and CEO of Autodesk, a leading maker of software for engineers and archi-tects in Sausalito, California: "I think that women in corporate America are still a generation away from real success."

Alas, the top men in corporate America appear to agree. A poll of 201 chief executives of the nation's largest companies, conducted exclusively for *Fortune* by the opinion research firm Clark Martire & Bartolomeo, reveals that only 16% believe it is

[1]Article by Anne B. Fisher. From *Fortune* 126/6:44+S 21 '92. Copyright © 1992 by Time, Inc. Reprinted with permission.

"very likely" or "somewhat likely" that they could be succeeded by a female CEO within the next decade. And only 18% think it's "very likely" that even after 20 years a woman would be picked to run their companies.

Why? The CEOs in our survey cite a host of reasons, but the biggest barrier, as a few of them admit, is an irrational one—plain and simple discrimination. Notes John H. Bryan, 56, CEO of Sara Lee: "I'm not sure there's a lot that women can do about it. They're already working hard and are very qualified. It shouldn't be this way, but too many senior managers, and particularly CEOs, tend to want to pass their jobs along to someone who's the image and likeness of themselves." John Nelson, 48, who heads Norwest Colorado, a bank holding company, agrees: "The problem with women advancing has more to do with men than with women. Men have dragged their feet."

Thanks for the honesty, guys, but that's pretty discouraging news. And coming during an election year in which, incredibly, some conservative politicians and leaders of the religious right are openly or implicitly condemning the very notion that women *should* work outside the home, it's enough to make even the most optimistic female executive despair. That would be wrong, however, because better days *are* coming.

True, progress has been painfully slow, and there has even been some backsliding. Susan Lowance, director of senior executive programs at MIT's Sloan School of Management, points out that the executive-training seminars run by U.S. business schools—an indispensable credential for future CEOs in many companies—are almost as exclusively a male preserve as Bohemian Grove. Enrollment in these programs nationwide is just 5% female, after peaking at 8% in the late 1980s. "Companies were trying a little harder, for a while, to develop senior women managers," Lowance explains. "But the recession scotched that. In tough times, top management prefers to entrust the risks that accompany decision-making at the highest levels to a known quantity—meaning someone like themselves. A man."

Here's more bad news: The Department of Labor's latest report on the limits to promotion of women at 94 major government contractors finds that few are being groomed for senior-level jobs. "The glass ceiling in most companies is a lot lower than we thought it was," says Labor Secretary Lynn Martin. "And too few women are getting the training they need to move up."

Nor have women managers achieved paycheck parity with

men. Among all females with full-time jobs, the much publicized wage gap between the sexes keeps shrinking. On average, a woman now earns about 74 cents for every dollar a man brings home, up from 65 cents a decade ago. Those relative gains reflect the fact that women are better educated and hold more highly skilled positions than ever before.

What's frustrating is that at the same level of management, the typical woman's pay is lower than her male colleague's—even when she has the exact same qualifications, works just as many years, relocates just as often, provides the main financial support for her family, takes no time off for personal reasons, and wins the same number of promotions to comparable jobs. That discouraging conclusion comes from a new study of 1,029 managers at 20 *Fortune 500* companies across eight industries. Over five years ending in 1989, women managers' pay increased 54%, their male counterparts' 65%.

Says Linda Stroh, 44, one of the study's co-authors, who teaches in the Institute of Industrial Relations at Loyola University in Chicago: "The disparity probably comes partly from the lingering and often unconscious perception that women are going to leave to have babies. But the women managers we studied were in the work force to stay and had done all the right stuff. It still wasn't enough."

Even so, most of the available data support the notion that, on balance, women in the workplace undeniably are advancing. To a man—and that's what they all are—the CEOs polled by *Fortune* say over the past five years the number of female middle managers at their companies has either increased (92%) or stayed about the same (8%). As for female officers, 62% of chief executives say their number rose as well. Insists Richard Deihl, 64, chairman of H. F. Ahmanson & Co., a big California mortgage lender: "Women are already moving up into higher and higher positions. We should at least see a woman chief operating officer here well before 20 years from now."

Labor Department statistics support this upbeat forecast. Using a broad-gauge definition of "manager" that includes everybody from the head of a fast food restaurant to a CEO, Labor reports that about 41% of U.S. managers were female as of mid-1991, up from 32% in 1983.

Fortune's own research suggests that a similar though smaller increase occurred in the number of top female managers. To see if America's business leaders were really walking their talk on this subject, we commissioned Directorship, a research and consulting firm in Westport, Connecticut, to comb the 1986 and 1991 annual reports of the companies whose bosses had answered our CEO poll. Its task: to tally the number of women who held senior positions in those two base years. We defined "senior" as a job within three levels of management of the chief executive's office. In the case of staff, that would encompass a chief financial officer or his equal, a company comptroller and his counterparts, and finally, say, someone like the head of the accounting staff. Among line officers, the three tiers might stretch from president to a division head.

Of this select group, 4.8% in 1991 turned out to be women. Think that's small? Go back five years, to 1986: Only 2.9% of senior managers were then female. Gazers at the half-empty part of glasses will quickly complain that roughly 5% is still a scant one-tenth the number of female managers we would have if women's presence in the executive suite matched their representation in the rest of the workplace. (Women now account for nearly half all full-time U.S. workers.) An optimist, of course, would applaud a rise of nearly 60% in just five years.

Most important, evidence abounds that women's secondclass citizenship in corporate America is finally about to be upgraded. Sex discrimination is already less of an obstacle in some industries than in others. High-tech and service companies, for example, are generally more inclined to promote women than old-line manufacturers in businesses like steel and autos.

One important agent of change will be demographics. Restructurings and layoffs have produced a surplus of skilled, experienced managers of both sexes. But rock-bottom birth rates in the early and middle 1970s guarantee that later in this decade and well into the next one, not enough boy babybusters will be there to fill the new managerial jobs that the economy will generate. Any business that wants to stay competitive will have to hire, train, and reward women.

Another demographic factor is the increasing prevalence of two-career marriages. Ellen Galinsky, co-president of a nonprofit New York City research and consulting group, the Families and Work Institute, often conducts focus groups with men in their 20s and 30s. "These men are almost all in dual-career households, and they have a totally different perspective from their fathers' generation," she notes. "They empathize far more with conflicts between family and work responsibilities, since they know first-hand what it's like to have no full-time help tending the home fires. They quite often say to me, 'These guys upstairs who are running things just don't *understand*.'"

Galinsky believes that as the current crop of thirtysomethings ascend to positions of power, companies' cultures are bound to become more flexible—and less insistent that a valued manager choose, in effect, between a child and a promotion. Jill Elikann Barad, 41, who in July [1990] was named president and chief operating officer of Mattel, the $1.6-billion-a-year toymaker, shares that faith in generational change. When told the results of *Fortune's* CEO poll, she dismissed as "ridiculous" the notion that women must expect to wait 20 more years to become chief executives. She says: "I don't know how these guys can say that. Maybe they won't be the ones making the decision."

Finally, there's the "pipeline" argument. For at least ten years we've all been hearing that while there aren't yet enough qualified women, as their number and experience increase, more will reach the top. Fully 64% of CEOs in *Fortune's* poll attribute women's absence from the executive suites in large part to lack of experience. "We've always joked that it takes 30 years to be allowed to empty the wastebaskets around here," says Charles A. Corry, 60, chairman of USX Corp. "It took me 21 years and 12 job changes to become a vice president. It's the same for women. It takes time." Robert C. Winters, 60, CEO of Prudential, agrees: "Women should persist, endure, hang in. The wave is really crest-high now. Women are making a mark, but they have to keep up the good work."

It's been a wearisome slog, but a light is now glimmering at the end of the pipeline. The Bureau of Labor Statistics reports that there are 6.1 million female managers in the U.S., up from about 3.5 million in 1983. These women, many of whom are in their early 30s to mid-40s, are the first generation to accumulate the same education, experience, and expectations as their male counterparts, and to find strength in their considerable numbers. Says MIT's Susan Lowance: "If many women are ever to reach the top of corporations, it's the ones in that big middle-management group who are going to do it." Labor Secretary Martin expects those middle managers to push hard for recognition. "A lot of us thought our pioneering days were over," she says, "but they aren't."

That's why the smartest companies are devoting ever more

time and resources to broadening and developing the talented female middle managers they have already hired. Hardly any of the CEOs polled by *Fortune*—only 8%—think women lack the aggressiveness or determination to scale the corporate heights. And just 5% said that women should be more willing than they are to relocate for a promotion, an issue that some studies have suggested is keeping good female managers down. But nearly half insisted that the reason it will take two decades for a female to rise to the top of their companies is that women managers are still too concentrated in fields such as communications and human resources, which rarely if ever lead upward.

"It really isn't a question of what else women should be doing. It's a question of what *companies* should be doing to ensure that women are getting the opportunities men get," says William Ruckelshaus, 60, chairman of Browning-Ferris Industries. Even in relatively nonsexist industries like retailing, some CEOs think there's much to be done. "We have to step up our commitment to exposing women to different dimensions of the business," says Allen Questrom, 51, chairman of Federated Department Stores. "Management has a clear responsibility to prepare women for broadbased roles."

Toward that end, dozens of corporate colossi, from AT&T to Johnson & Johnson to Xerox, have hired full-time "diversity managers," charged by top management to make the workplace more hospitable to talent of either sex and all colors. In some cases this is pure tinsel and tokenism, but for many companies it's a hard-nosed business strategy. Says Aetna Life & Casualty CEO Ronald Compton, 59, who is largely responsible for the fact that roughly half his company's managers are now women: "I'm not doing this out of the goodness of my heart. I'm selfish. I want the very best people I can get. A lot of them happen to be women." No diversity campaign will succeed without that kind of blessing from the top.

Alarmed that turnover among female engineers and salespeople was twice as high as among men, chemical giant Monsanto hired a consultant to do exit interviews with departing women. Most said they'd had better offers from competitors or planned to start their own firms. "There is a glass ceiling at Monsanto," admits vice president of administration Michael Miller. "We're trying to break it." How? Like many another company with a formal diversity program, Monsanto now evaluates—and pays—its managers partly on the basis of how carefully they identify, train, and promote women.

Accounting behemoth Arthur Andersen recruited Joseph Stokes, a psychology professor at the University of Illinois at Chicago, to help it work out a diversity program. Stokes says that to ensure that women get more of the broad experience required to rise to officer status, companies must stop assuming that men are automatically more willing than women to leap across divisional boundaries for new assignments. "More companies need to ask both women and men what their long-term career goals are, what kinds of jobs would interest them most, whether they'd consider an overseas transfer, and so on," says he. "And then use that laundry list—which is a kind of blueprint of a person's ambitions—and develop everyone accordingly."

Beyond allowing qualified women an equal chance at the same jobs men get, diversity-minded companies are trying to re-cast their cultures so that old attitudinal hurdles don't trip up women who might otherwise be gold medalists. Nancy Hamlin, president of consulting firm Hamlin Fox in Marblehead, Massachusetts, has spent 25 years as an adviser on gender issues to General Electric, Hewlett-Packard, Digital Equipment Corp., Fleet Bank, and the U.S. Coast Guard. She says that even in the best-intentioned and most progressive companies, women are usually kept out of the informal channels of information, where important decisions sometimes crystallize. Female managers, for example, are left behind when their male peers go out to lunch, or to a sporting event, or on a good old-fashioned pub crawl. "Men don't do this on purpose," Hamlin says. "They just don't *think* about it."

She and other diversity experts add that, since the Anita Hill–Clarence Thomas debacle, fear and confusion have multiplied. As she says, "Male executives will think, 'Hmmm, wouldn't it be easier, and safer, to take this business trip, or go to that client dinner, with another guy?'" But the most pervasive problem, and perhaps the most intractable one, is that a lifetime of social conditioning has trained many men to think of women as sweethearts, wives, daughters, secretaries—not as equal colleagues. Muses Hamlin: "It's hard to completely re-socialize people."

Hard, but not impossible. Short of waiting for the diehard chauvinists to retire or threatening to fire them if they can't get with the program, what can top management do? Monsanto's diversity effort is typical. The company holds workshops, run by consultants Pope & Associates, designed to expose and dismantle workers' prejudices. About 5,000 Monsanto employees have attended the six-day sessions, and more are signed up to do so.

Keri Bauch-Sparks, 37, an information systems manager at a Monsanto chemical plant in Sauget, Illinois, has been through this drill twice in the past four years. "Some men's initial reaction to it is defensive. They think it's going to be a lot of finger-pointing," she says. "But the idea is to improve communications for everybody. Once people see that, they're generally enthusiastic."

In one exercise, the moderator asks group members to write down every stereotypical notion about women they can think of, and the answers are posted on the walls for discussion. One widespread perception among men, which comes up repeatedly, is that women make lousy candidates for promotion because they always put their personal lives, particularly their children, ahead of work. "When you see this stuff up on flip charts around the room, it gets people thinking," says Bauch-Sparks. "Society has been telling us these things for years, but do we necessarily believe they're true?" Slowly but certainly, perceptions at Monsanto are changing, and that seems to be encouraging ambitious women to stick around. Turnover is down, and a second round of exit interviews this summer unearthed far fewer responses marked by frustration and bitterness.

Rare is the company intent on keeping its best female employees and managers that doesn't have some kind of work-family program—a bit of jargon that encompasses everything from day care centers to programs that counsel employees on how to cope with the problems of elderly parents. All share the same purpose: to bolster employee productivity by eliminating some of the distractions that family life inevitably imposes on single parents and two-income couples.

Since 1971 the number of large U.S. employers that provide some kind of day-care assistance has grown from 11 to nearly 4,000. Now many companies are going much further. Kraft-General Foods offers the 2,000 employees at its headquarters in White Plains, New York, a smorgasbord of work-family benefits, including nearby company-subsidized day care centers, extended parental leaves, and vacation time available by the half-day.

Irene Rosenfeld, 39, is executive vice president in charge of the $1-billion-a-year beverage division that makes Kool-Aid and Country Time lemonade. She's also the mother of two young daughters, and she calls the work-family program "terrific."

These new policies and services are not for women only. Says Rosenfeld: "Women's issues are rapidly becoming work force issues, and companies that best address them will win in the marketplace." Her own division is winning handily, with double-digit earnings increases in each of the past five years.

About one-third of chief executives in *Fortune's* survey say they've noticed that women's careers often stall out for lack of the kind of informal advice and sponsorship men get from one another. Some companies are trying to remedy that with mentoring programs that pair promising women, nominated by their department heads, with senior executives who proffer one-on-one career counseling. San Francisco-based Pacific Bell started its mentoring drive in late 1989, so the second batch of about 35 female protégées are now nearing the end of their two-year program. What exactly does a mentor do? Consider the experience of D. J. Hulet, 36. She started out in sales 15 years ago, moved up steadily, and in 1990 was assigned mentor John Seymour, 48, vice president and general manager of Pacific Bell's Orange-Riverside division.

Perhaps not surprisingly, she and he view her strengths and weaknesses somewhat differently. "I'm very candid, and I speak my mind," says Hulet. "Other managers have told me, 'You know, if you did the same things you're doing and you were a guy, you'd be OK.'" Really? Seymour explains: "Some people here saw her as very bright but too aggressive. In my opinion there's no such thing as too aggressive. But you do have to learn how to approach people in a way that doesn't create enemies." Seymour coached her on how to influence people without alienating them, manifestly a valuable skill: Hulet was promoted in mid-1991 to regional marketing manager for Los Angeles.

As more women attain high positions, they are reaching out to guide their younger counterparts—sometimes those still in school. A University of Pennsylvania alumnae group called the Trustees' Council of Penn Women, currently headed by First Interstate Bancorp senior vice president Pamela Reis, gives female seniors and business school students a list of about 70 distinguished women they can call for career advice or information. The council also runs a "shadowing" program that lets students spend a workday with a woman executive for a close-up peek at the real world. Constance Duckworth, 37, a partner in fixed-income securities at Goldman Sachs in Chicago, spent time this summer with a 21-year-old Wharton finance student. The two plan to stay in touch. "This is something I didn't have when I was starting out in business," says Duckworth. "It's an 'old-girls' network,' in an embryonic stage."

"Women do need to do more networking," declares Autodesk Chairman Carol Bartz. As a stellar senior executive at Sun Microsystems before taking her current job, Bartz met often with groups of women in the company for brown-bag lunches and tried to make herself available to advise anyone who sought her insights. "At some point I realized, 'Hey, these people are looking up to me,' and my first reaction was, 'I don't have *time* for this,'" she recalls. "But I decided I had to take the responsibility to help pave the way for others—including my daughter, who's 4."

What advice does she give women who aspire to the top job? Like the chief executives in *Fortune's* poll, Bartz believes that women often don't get a wide enough range of experience. "You have to step out of the pack and take risks, even be willing to jump completely out of your element if that's what it takes," she says. It helps, she adds, to start as early as possible. Bartz knows whereof she speaks. Seventeen years ago, while still in her 20s, she quit a comfortable job as a systems analyst at 3M in Atlanta after a marketing executive at headquarters told her the company would never let a woman sell computers.

That fellow is probably kicking himself now. In 1987, with some trepidation, Bartz took over Sun's federal government sales division, an area of the business that was not only entirely alien to her but was populated largely, she says, with "cigar-chomping ex-defense contractors." In just two years under her management, the unit's revenues jumped from $21 million to $124 million.

"There's still a lot of folklore out there about what women can and can't do," observes Kraft–General Foods' Irene Rosenfeld. "But don't ever believe you can't do something until you've tried it." In an apt metaphor, given her position, she adds: "Just do your job brilliantly, and sooner or later the cream will rise to the top."

Over and over again, female and male managers urge women to set career goals and work out a specific plan for achieving them. Hugh McColl Jr., 57, is CEO of NationsBank, the holding company in Charlotte, North Carolina, formed by the recent merger of NCNB and C&S/Sovran. McColl told *Fortune's* pollsters: "Women have to push harder. They often feel that things will be done fairly, whereas men don't believe that, and in reality it's often not the case. So women must ask their bosses what's needed to get to the next level. They then need to make sure they get those opportunities, and ask for feedback every step of the way."

But while you're pushing, keep a stiff upper lip. Mary Herbert, 41, vice president and director of quality for international operations at Motorola, has talked extensively with her female colleagues about their careers. "You do have to go to management and say, 'Here's what I think I can do; here's why; let me try it,'" she says. "But from what I've seen, women who have had a chip on their shoulder—who basically said, 'I should get this job because there are no women at this level of the company'—those are the ones who aren't getting anywhere at all." (See following story.)

The surest way to ascend, of course, is to be so good they can't overlook you. Jill Barad won the No. 2 spot at Mattel largely because as head of the girls' toy division she had overseen a doubling of worldwide sales of Barbie dolls in under four years, to nearly $1 billion. She dismisses the notion that women are at any special disadvantage in business—at least, not if they're smart, hard working, and imaginative. "One day soon, it isn't going to matter anymore what sex anyone is," she says. "It'll come down to a question of who delivers the goods. Performance is what counts."

Hazel O'Leary, 55, an executive vice president at Northern States Power in Minneapolis, agrees: "Whatever you're asked to do, make sure you do a better job of it than the man next to you." But while you're at it, don't neglect to form friendships. "Without losing your own personality, it's important to be part of the prevailing corporate culture," she says. "At this company, it's golf. I've resisted learning to play golf all my life, but I finally had to admit I was missing something that way." O'Leary has bought a set of clubs and tees up with an instructor on weekends.

The best reason for believing that more women will be in charge before long is that in a ferociously competitive global economy, no company can afford to waste valuable brainpower simply because it's wearing a skirt. That isn't easy for some folks to accept. "Dealing with change is always painful," notes William Boyle, a Monsanto plant manager who is a big believer in the company's diversity-training programs. "But the days when any U.S. company could stand pat, do things the same old way, and say, 'Gosh, look how good we are'—those days are gone."

Happily for women in corporate America, radical change has a way of favoring the underdog. Says Jane White, author of the forthcoming book *A Few Good Women: Breaking the Barriers to Top Management*: "I think we're living in a fantastic time. The ferment that is happening now will push the barricades down." For that to occur, it's crucial that the brightest and best women not become discouraged. As White puts it, "If you're going to be in the forefront of a revolution, you have to keep taking the flak until it's won."

CREATING CHANGE BY COMMITTEE[2]

"Construction has always been an elusive field for women. Even now we account for only about 2 percent of all of the high-paid, skilled-labor workers. To this day, women can be kept out of the industry and off job sites by contractors who use what are called "best-effort" programs. What this means is, "Be sure and cover your ass with documentation. Then go out, make some calls, and when nobody comes through, you can say you made your best effort."

Those women who *have* been hired often find themselves surrounded by hostility. In one case, a carpenter's apprentice who asked for and received separate toilet facilities was locked out of them by her male colleagues, who also vandalized the facilities to make their point. In another case, an asbestos worker was laid off after informing her employer that she was pregnant and requesting a safer job. Firms can no longer afford or tolerate this type of behavior. But recruiting women in the building trades is increasingly important because of women's increasing role in the labor force—it's in everyone's best interest to hire and train them now. To do that, I realized I would have to create an atmosphere of cooperation, not enforced compliance.

Laying the Foundation

I started out as a high school teacher, but in 1976, at the urging of my friend Richard Stein, I joined his fledgling company. I got in on the ground floor, so to speak, and rose to become

[2]Article from *Working Woman* 17/4: 29–30 Ap '92. Copyright © 1992 by Working Woman, Inc. Reprinted with permission.

president in 1991. When I first asked our contractors to open jobs
to women, they said they'd love to but the unions didn't have
many women in their ranks. The unions, in turn, said they'd love
to admit more women but the contractors didn't want to hire
them. There was a lot of finger-pointing, which told me that
someone familiar with the needs of all groups involved had to
step in and put pressure on them.

I understood both sides, but there are a lot of contractors and
unions in this town, and I knew that Stein & Company couldn't do
it alone. So, with the blessing of Richard Stein, I created the
Female Employment Initiative (FEI), a committee of 10 women
from local contracting and nonprofit groups. The members are
paid as consultants by Stein & Company to encourage women to
seek jobs with the potential to improve their economic status—
with higher wages, better benefits, a wider variety of work schedules and more opportunities for advancement. FEI would not
only train women who wanted to be construction workers, but it
would also make sure that lewd graffiti, pornography, isolation,
aggression and other forms of harassment did not make the job
site difficult or impossible for them to work at. FEI met frequently with the builders as well.

I found committee members among the ranks of Stein &
Company's employees, the Chicago Urban League, the Hispanic
American Construction Industry Association, affirmative-action
consultants and training and placement organizations, like the
Chicago Women in Trades, the Coalition for United Community
Action and the Midwest Women's Center. I wanted people who
were in touch with as many people in the community as possible.
At first, many members doubted that the idea would work, since
they were used to seeking change through the courts. But I told
them that in the long run, our efforts would be more effective if
we worked from within. They were hopeful because FEI brought
them into the system.

A Beer With the Foreman

The committee's first big test came in 1988, just after Stein &
Company was hired to build the $153 million Ralph H. Metcalfe
Federal Building in Chicago. FEI sent representatives to meet
with the contractors and began accepting job applications from
women. Each woman's job experience went into a database, and
FEI presented all their qualifications during meetings with the

general contractor. To make the women feel comfortable about
signing on, FEI held orientation sessions at the job site. We also
gave women a tour and invited them to talk to apprentices and
journeyworkers.

Once construction began, FEI made sure that women were
getting a fair shot at things like overtime pay by monitoring daily
head counts. In all, about 60 percent of the 65 contractors on the
project agreed to hire women, who in the end made up 85 of the
500 tradespeople working on the building.

To guard against harassment, we gave the women the phone
number of an FEI coordinator, who protected their anonymity.
One of the first complaints we received was over the lack of private toilet facilities. Above street level, the stalls were booths without tops, which allowed objects to be tossed in. New ones were
immediately installed that had canvas tops. This paved the way
for separate changing facilities every four floors at our next job
site.

We posted bulletin boards with information about such things
as where to buy boots and protective clothing. We also spoke with
workers to find out how it was going. Interestingly, it wasn't just
the women who wanted to talk. Sometimes a man would ask
whom his sister-in-law could call about a job.

FEI communicated with foremen, too, and committee representatives took them out for a beer on a regular basis. Although I
don't tend to get involved at this level, because it would change
the dynamic of the meeting, I did urge the group to hear the
foremen out. When you sit down after hours with people like that
and try to understand their problems, they're going to be more
likely to help you with yours.

Building Up the Program

To say that women are now fully accepted in the building
trades would be an overstatement. For example, there were problems that popped up on the Metcalfe project that involved the
reluctance of men to accept a woman's place in the pecking order.
One woman, who was a fourth-year apprentice, was given a full-
fledged skilled job when the work started. But later a first-year
man replaced her, and she was relegated to housekeeping chores
that he should have been doing. On the other hand, a woman who
was a first-year apprentice refused to do entry-level chores she
considered too menial. The conflicts cut both ways, and we didn't

want supervisors to evaluate all women workers on the basis of three or four. We feel that we accomplished that by getting so many women on the job.

Affirmative action is now a part of every project Stein & Company takes on. We set no quotas, but we make it clear up front that bidders are expected to support our social goals. Since the Metcalfe job, FEI has been involved in several projects, including U.S. Gypsum's headquarters, which will be finished in June and has employed 75 women. We're about to break ground on two others in Chicago—a professional-sports arena and a convention center. I expect that 75 to 90 women will be hired for the former and 120 to 150 for the latter.

It has been especially gratifying that male construction workers have become some of our biggest supporters. One formerly skeptical foreman came up to me recently and said, "Women aren't going away. If they want to learn, let's teach them so they can be really good." But what inspires me most is when I'm talking to a woman on the job and she says, "I can't tell you how good it feels when I bring the kids downtown and point up to a 60-story building and say, 'I built that.'"

THE WAGE WAR AGAINST WOMEN[3]

Like many women who came of age after the women's movement had begun, Vikki Soreo-Yasher took her equality at work for granted. Sure, she was aware that women sometimes had problems in the workplace, but she hadn't experienced any herself.

That all changed when Soreo-Yasher, a property manager in Cleveland, announced to her employer, First Office Management, a national real-estate company, that she was pregnant. In her eighth month, a week before her scheduled leave, Soreo-Yasher walked into her office and found her boss waiting for her. "He said he wanted to go over things in preparation for my imminent leave," she recalls. Then, according to Soreo-Yasher, as they

[3]Article by Michele Morris. From *Working Mother* 15:60–3 Je '92. Reprinted with permission.

were wrapping up the meeting, he announced that she had been replaced by someone else. "I couldn't believe it. I almost fainted," she says. "I asked him 'How can you do this?' He said that I had a big job and he couldn't leave it open for eight weeks. He had already hired someone from Cincinnati, and he said he only wished I'd be around to train my replacement—who was a man."

Once she recovered from her shock, Soreo-Yasher called her husband and then a hotline operated by 9to5, National Association of Working Women, which counsels women who run into unfair practices at work. Convinced that she had a legitimate case against her employer, she filed a formal complaint with the U.S. Equal Employment Opportunity Commission, charging that the firm had fired her solely because she was pregnant, a blatant case of sex discrimination. Frances Lewis, vice president of publications for Equity, the parent company of First Office Management, refused to comment on Soreo-Yasher's case, but told *Working Mother,* "Our company does not discharge people because of maternity. In my ten years with the company, I've taken two maternity leaves."

Last October, while the EEOC was investigating Soreo-Yasher's case, she was still unemployed and home with her baby. Along with millions of other Americans, she was riveted by the televised hearings in which law professor Anita Hill accused Supreme Court nominee Clarence Thomas of sexual harassment. Like many working women, Soreo-Yasher was outraged by the condescending and hostile way the all-male Senate Judiciary Committee treated Hill. That scene was a turning point for her; she decided to pursue her own case more aggressively. She hired a private attorney to sue her former employer for sex discrimination. (First Office Management will not discuss the case while it is in litigation.)

The chances of women such as Soreo-Yasher winning their cases just went up considerably, say labor lawyers. That's because late last fall [1991] Congress passed a tough new civil rights law, which strengthens women's rights on the job. "The new law puts stronger teeth in antidiscrimination laws for women," says Isabelle Katz Pinzler, director of the Women's Rights Project of the American Civil Liberties Union, which is based in New York City.

Indeed, the Civil Rights Act of 1991—and other recent court decisions—has given women new clout in the workplace. When women are treated unfairly on the job, they can now:
- Collect monetary damages when they win a case.
- Ask that their case be tried before a jury.

• Sue as a group when an employer violates the rights of a number of women in a workplace.

• Ask the courts to judge their cases through the eyes of a "reasonable woman" instead of the long-held legal standard based on how a "reasonable man" would see the facts.

• Win a case without as much effort; the new law puts more of the burden of proof on the employer, rather than the employee.

Taken together, these changes reverse a growing trend in court decisions that had made it increasingly difficult for a woman to win a sex-discrimination suit—and impossible for her to impose any serious penalty on an employer who violated her rights—no matter how badly she had been treated on the job.

The new law, along with recent legal decisions, is big news for you and your co-workers, since women still suffer widespread discrimination in the workplace. For many women, it often arrives in the form of sexual harassment—from uninvited advances to lewd posters on office walls. For pregnant women and new mothers, it shows up as pregnancy discrimination. And for women who have excelled in their careers, it's the glass ceiling—an invisible barrier that keeps women from the executive suite.

High Cost of Unfair Workplaces

Whatever its guise, such discrimination takes a toll on women's morale, productivity, opportunities to advance and, quite painfully, on their paychecks. The fact that women still earn far less than men can be largely attributed to the long-term effects of unfair practices on the job. Women's labor is still not valued as highly as men's: Women earn only 71 cents for every dollar the average man earns.

Many labor experts blame the pay gap on the fact that women have always been hired for less than their male peers—and then kept at a lower salary throughout their careers. The median annual salary of women ages 40 to 44 is now $22,000 for full-time work. According to the Institute for Women's Policy Research, that's about the same salary a 25-to-29-year-old man earns as he is just starting out in his career. "A woman with a four-year college degree now earns about the same as a man with a high-school diploma," says Pamela Hughes of the American Association of University Women.

Last year, the EEOC received more than 29,000 complaints of sex discrimination. As the new civil rights law takes effect, lawyers predict an upsurge in cases. "The changes in the law will help women come forward," says Debra L. Raskin, a partner at Vladeck, Waldman, Elias & Engelhard, a New York City law firm specializing in employment law.

New Muscle in the Courts

Many observers say that the most important aspect of the new law is that it imposes serious consequences on employers who treat women unfairly. Under the old civil rights law, passed back in 1964, women were entitled only to back pay and reinstatement in their old job.

Even in the most egregious cases, the employers escaped unscathed. Consider what happened to Helen Brooms, an industrial nurse who was harassed on the job. On numerous occasions, her supervisor made sexual overtures, showed her pornographic photographs and made lewd comments. During one incident, when Brooms resisted, he even vowed to kill her! While she was trying to evade him, she fell down a flight of stairs. Besides being disabled, she suffered severe depression. In *Brooms v. Regal Tube Co.*, the court found her civil rights had indeed been violated. She was awarded some back pay but nothing for her physical or emotional suffering.

Over the last few years, women's rights activists have tried to get more teeth in the law. But it was hard to stir much interest in Congress—until the Clarence Thomas confirmation hearings last fall. The furor that ensued was just the fuel needed to pass the Civil Rights Act of 1991. Now women can sue to recover the financial, medical and emotional costs of discrimination, as well as punitive damages. "The women of America have Anita Hill to thank," says the American Civil Liberties Union's (ACLU) Pinzler. "Before the Thomas hearings, the civil rights bill was dead in the water."

The new law also gives women the right to a jury trial, an important tool since juries are usually more sympathetic than judges to complaints filed by workers. A discrimination case that was decided recently by a jury at the state level has been widely cited as what may happen across the U.S. as more women begin to sue under the new federal law—Barbara Soggs, an American Airlines employee who charged that she had been passed over for a job in favor of a less-qualified, less-experienced man, sued her employer under New York State human rights law. The jury awarded her $7.1 million in damages.

The 1991 civil rights law does have its limitations, however. Congressional supporters had to agree to a cap on damages available to women in discrimination cases: Companies with more than 500 employees are liable for no more than $300,000; the cap is even lower for smaller firms. Still, the right to garner *any* damages is a big improvement for working women in this country.

The new law also reverses a troubling trend of court decisions that had gradually eroded women's rights in the workplace. In a key decision in 1989, the Supreme Court ruled in the case of *Wards Cove Packing Co. v. Atonio* that employees must take on the almost impossible burden of proving that an employer's unfair practices had no business justification. Thus, if a woman was fired from a job after she announced she was pregnant, she had to prove that the company had no business reason for her layoff—a nearly hopeless task for a woman not privy to the decision-making process at her company. The new civil rights law shifts the burden of proof back to the employer—if a firm claims that there was a legitimate business reason for an action such as a layoff, the firm now has to present all relevant papers to prove it.

A Reasonable Woman

The changes in the civil rights law are not the only new forces on women's side. There are other important developments that have strengthened women's rights. A woman's point of view has also gained clout in legal circles. Historically courts have relied on the "reasonable man" standard to decide cases; that is, a judge or jury must decide what a reasonable man would make of the facts of the case. That standard does not always work well for women—a man simply may not understand, for example, what it feels like to be a woman in an office where men hang up nudie calendars or make lewd comments.

But last year a circuit court accepted a new point of view. The judges ruled that incidents of sexual harassment must be judged on the basis of whether a "reasonable woman" would find the acts offensive, intimidating or hostile.

The plaintiff in this ground-breaking case, *Ellison v. Brady*, was Kerry Ellison, an IRS worker in California. One day one of her co-workers, a man whose desk was 20 feet from hers, started asking her out for drinks and lunch. Even though she made it clear that she wasn't interested, he continued to bug her, writing her long love letters and bizarre notes that made repeated sexual references. When the harassment escalated, Ellison complained to management, who moved the man to another office. Six months later, without notifying Ellison, they allowed him to return. Terrified of her harasser, she asked for a transfer and then brought suit. The court eventually decided in her favor, ruling that any reasonable woman in Ellison's shoes would have felt frightened.

One other important court case has also added a weapon to women's arsenal of defense against discrimination. Women can now sue as a group—which gives them far more power. A federal district judge in Minnesota recently permitted a group of female iron-mine workers to pursue their lawsuit against the Eveleth Taconite Company as a class action suit, the first time it's been done. "The ruling gives all women faced with sexual harassment a powerful new tool," says Paul Sprenger, the women's attorney.

Companies Take Notice

While it's exhilarating that all these things are coalescing on the legal front, women's advocates are hoping that the courtroom victories will be felt in women's paychecks. There is some evidence that there is already reason to cheer—a growing number of firms are revising their policies and creating programs to end discrimination—and to open more of their top jobs to women.

The day after Anita Hill's testimony, AT&T's chairman, Robert E. Allen, placed the company's entire sexual-harassment policy on its electronic network to make it clear that the communications giant would not tolerate unfair treatment of women. Other large corporations put out press releases to advise their workers and the general public that they intend to combat any illtreatment of women. American Express issued a memorandum reaffirming the company's sexual-harassment policy and guidelines. Freada Klein, a Cambridge, Massachusetts, management consultant, predicts that within a year or two 90 percent of *Fortune 500* companies will offer employees special training about sexual harassment.

Some firms are also trying to smash the glass ceiling that keeps women from the most senior jobs. Many labor experts believe women are held back from top jobs because of subtle discrimination that occurs at this level—women don't fit in, they're not familiar with the jargon of sports and the military, they don't play golf or hang out in the men's clubs. So women find themselves inexplicably stalled in their careers. According to a Labor Department study of nine *Fortune 1000* companies, women represent 37.2 percent of all employees and 16.9 percent of managers. But a mere 6.6 percent of executive-level managers are women.

"The glass ceiling is really sex discrimination that hinders women at every step and every level of the work force," insists Judith L. Lichtman, president of the Women's Legal Defense Fund, a Washington, D.C.-based advocacy group. "Discrimination prevents most women from reaching positions where they can even *see* the glass ceiling."

Other companies have set up formal mentor programs to ensure that women get the help and feedback crucial to career development. Du Pont, for example, has designated a staffer to specifically focus on the careers of women and minorities and play the role of advocate. If a division is looking for a new person, Bob Brandt, manager of affirmative action and upward mobility, will be brought into the discussion. "I suggest female candidates who might not have been considered. I keep asking the question 'Why not?' to try to break down the stereotypical thinking of what a woman can do," Brandt explains.

Still, many women feel that more needs to be done to ensure their rights, and a few are already pressing beyond the new rights won by the 1991 Civil Rights Act. Eight women of the Stroh Brewery Company in Detroit recently sued the firm for sexual harassment, charging they had to work in an environment openly hostile to women.

In such a male-dominated industry, that might not seem so unusual. But these women added a new charge—they claimed that a series of Stroh's commercials, some of which featured the big-breasted "Swedish bikini team," revealed management's generally disrespectful attitude toward women—which furthers their own ill-treatment in the workplace. The company has defended its ads as simple entertainment protected by the First Amendment's guarantee of free speech. "If men in the workplace say women are tits and ass, the law says that's sexual harassment," says Lori Peterson, the Minneapolis lawyer representing the Stroh employees. "If it's multiplied by a $19 million ad campaign, they say it's free speech. We intend to challenge that view. We contend that this advertising is just one more indication that the company sanctions sexism." If these women win, it will be yet another landmark for women's rights in the workplace.

Whatever the outcome for these workers, women have won some key victories. Such efforts should improve working conditions and salary for all women. "Last year was an energizing year for American women. They're galvanized," says Barbara Otto of

9to5, National Association of Working Women. "Women have finally made the connection that what happens in Washington, D.C., affects what happens to them on the job every day."

WORKING WOMEN'S STAUNCHEST ALLIES: SUPPLY AND DEMAND[4]

Working women have plenty of problems in the workplace, as we were reminded so dramatically during the Clarence Thomas hearings. Yet those problems stand in stark contrast to women's rapid progress in occupations and earnings compared with men's since the late 1970s. The U.S. is getting much closer to granting equal pay for equal work, regardless of gender or family situation.

The proportion of married women who work has increased continuously: Now [1991], more than 60% of married women with young children hold jobs. Women in the 1970s and '80s entered many professions at a breathtaking pace. They make up some 40% of the students in schools of law, medicine, business, architecture, and journalism, and are a small but rapidly growing share of those majoring in engineering. The percentage of male college graduates going on to law school has actually fallen since 1970, while females in the legal profession have risen from a negligible share in the early '70s to almost 25% now.

Median earnings of women working full time were comparatively stable from 1960 to 1979, at about 59% of the earnings of men—which means a gender gap of about 41%. But then, as reported in the Census Bureau's *Money Income of Households, Families and Persons*, the gap began a steady fall, dropping below 30% in 1990. I expect it to continue to fall throughout this decade.

Even 30%, however, overstates the true gap, since female full-time workers put in about 10% fewer hours a week than male full-time workers, and they have less previous job experience. The gap between men and women working the same hours and with the same experience is well under 20%.

---

[4]Article by Gary S. Becker, Professor of Economics and Sociology, University of Chicago, from *Business Week* De 2 '91. Copyright © 1991 by McGraw-Hill, Inc. Reprinted with permission.

Lame Excuse

The most important reason for women's progress is their increasing presence in the labor force, as the nature of the family has changed. Birth rates have dropped more than 35% since the late 1950s, freeing women from child care duties. Rapid expansion in the number of jobs in the service sector has let women combine child care with part-time work and flexible schedules. The exploding number of divorces after the mid-1960s forced women with dependent children to earn a living and provided a warning to married women that they should be prepared to work in the event their marriages should break up. Young women who have entered professions and other skilled occupations during the 1970s and 1980s continue to advance into more responsible positions, even if a "glass ceiling" has kept most from getting to the very top.

Not long ago, some women lost their jobs when they married. Women employees were paid much less than men, sometimes because of outright discrimination rationalized by the lame excuse that they were not the main breadwinners. The atmosphere created by civil rights legislation and the women's movement help combat such policies. These were not, however, the main forces behind their progress, since the gender gap in earnings did not begin to decline until more than a decade and a half after passage of the far-reaching Civil Rights Act of 1964. Women advanced most rapidly during the Reagan and Bush Presidencies—surely no more active in civil rights enforcement than previous Administrations. Moreover, not all minority groups advanced during the 1980s: Black men fell a little further behind white men.

Women's substantial progress during the '80s helped muffle the call for more radical legislation to aid them. There is much less support now than a decade ago for the silly system of government wage-setting figured on the basis of "comparable worth," the inevitably arbitrary judgments of statisticians and bureaucrats about what the pay should be in different occupations. Rapid entry of women into prestigious occupations has also quieted the call for quotas. Even supporters concede quotas aren't really what they have in mind.

Mothers' Helper

Instead, the drive to aid women is concentrating on other kinds of intervention in labor markets. Current favorites are mandatory, unpaid leave for parents when children are born or get sick and mandatory child care facilities at work. Bills in Congress would make child care leave available to either parent, but the example of Sweden—which has a liberal leave system—suggests that almost all would be taken by women.

Forcing business to provide leave is both inefficient and unjust. It in effect discriminates against single persons and against married women and men with no children or with grown children. It's one thing to call for a gender-neutral productivity test for pay hikes and promotions, but another to make business give preference to persons with young children. And while the present proposals are mild, everyone knows they are only a first step toward the Swedish system of requiring full pay for employees on child care leave.

The law of supply and demand, along with civil rights legislation, is steadily improving the economic position of U.S. women. Extensive intervention in labor markets to help them is unwarranted and will do more harm than good in implementing the principles of equal pay and equal employment opportunities for equal work.

THE MYTH OF THE MISERABLE WORKING WOMAN[5]

If you believe what you read, working women are in big trouble—stressed out, depressed, sick, risking an early death from heart attacks, and so overcome with problems at home that they make inefficient employees at work.

In fact, just the opposite is true. As a research psychologist whose career has focused on women and a journalist-critic who has studied the behavior of the media, we have extensively surveyed the latest data and research and concluded that the public is being engulfed by a tidal wave of disinformation that has serious consequences for the life and health of every American woman. Since large numbers of women began moving into the work

[5]Article by Rosalind C. Barnett and Caryl Rivers. From *Working Woman* 17/2:62+ F '92. Copyright © 1992 by Working Woman, Inc. Reprinted with permission.

force in the 1970s, scores of studies on their emotional and physical health have painted a very clear picture: Paid employment provides substantial health *benefits* for women. These benefits cut across income and class lines; even women who are working because they have to—not because they want to—share in them.

There is a curious gap, however, between what these studies say and what is generally reported on television, radio, and in newspapers and magazines. The more the research shows work is good for women, the bleaker the media reports seem to become. Whether this bizarre state of affairs is the result of a backlash against women, as *Wall Street Journal* reporter Susan Faludi contends in her new book, *Backlash: The Undeclared War Against American Women* [1991], or of well-meaning ignorance, the effect is the same: Both the shape of national policy and the lives of women are at risk.

Too often, legislation is written and policies are drafted not on the basis of the facts but on the basis of what those in power believe to be the facts. Even the much-discussed *Workforce 2000* report, issued by the Department of Labor under the Reagan administration—hardly a hotbed of feminism—admitted that "most current policies were designed for a society in which men worked and women stayed home." If policies are skewed toward solutions that are aimed at reducing women's commitment to work, they will do more than harm women—they will damage companies, managers and the productivity of the American economy.

The Coronary That Wasn't

One reason the "bad news" about working women jumps to page one is that we're all too willing to believe it. Many adults today grew up at a time when soldiers were returning home from World War II and a way had to be found to get the women who replaced them in industry back into the kitchen. The result was a barrage of propaganda that turned at-home moms into saints and backyard barbecues and station wagons into cultural icons. Many of us still have that outdated postwar map inside our heads, and it leaves us more willing to believe the horror stories than the good news that paid employment is an emotional and medical plus.

In the 19th century it was accepted medical dogma that women should not be educated because the brain and the ovaries could not develop at the same time. Today it's PMS, the wrong math genes or rampaging hormones. Hardly anyone points out the dire predictions that didn't come true.

You may remember the prediction that career women would start having more heart attacks, just like men. But the Framingham Heart Study—a federally funded cardiac project that has been studying 10,000 men and women since 1948—reveals that working women are not having more heart attacks. They're not dying any earlier, either. Not only are women not losing their health advantages; the lifespan gap is actually widening. Only one group of working women suffers more heart attacks than other women: those in low-paying clerical jobs with many demands on them and little control over their work pace, who also have several children and little or no support at home.

As for the recent publicity about women having more problems with heart disease, much of it skims over the important underlying reasons for the increase—namely, that by the time they have a heart attack, women tend to be a good deal older (an average of 67, six years older than the average age for men), and thus frailer, than males who have one. Also, statistics from the National Institutes of Health show that coronary symptoms are treated less aggressively in women—fewer coronary bypasses, for example. In addition, most heart research is done on men, so doctors do not know as much about the causes—and treatment—of heart disease in women. None of these factors have anything to do with work.

But doesn't working put women at greater risk for stress-related illnesses? No. Paid work is actually associated with *reduced* anxiety and depression. In the early 1980s we reported in our book, *Lifeprints* (based on a National Science Foundation–funded study of 300 women), that working women were significantly higher in psychological well-being than those not employed. Working gave them a sense of mastery and control that home-making didn't provide. More recent studies echo our findings. For example:

• A 1989 report by psychologist Ingrid Waldron and sociologist Jerry Jacobs of Temple University on nationwide surveys of 2,392 white and 892 black women, conducted from 1977 to 1982, found that women who held both work and family roles reported better physical and mental health than homemakers.

• According to sociologists Elaine Wethington of Cornell University and Ronald Kessler of the University of Michigan, data from three years (1985 to 1988) of a continuing federally funded study of 745 married women in Detroit "clearly suggests that employment benefits women emotionally." Women who increase their participation in the labor force report lower levels of psychological distress; those who lessen their commitment to work suffer from higher distress.

• A University of California at Berkeley study published in 1990 followed 140 women for 22 years. At age 43, those who were homemakers had more chronic conditions than the working women and seemed more disillusioned and frustrated. The working mothers were in good health and seemed to be juggling their roles with success.

In sum, paid work offers women heightened self-esteem and enhanced mental and physical health. It's unemployment that's a major risk factor for depression in women.

Doing It All—And Doing Fine

This isn't true only for affluent women in good jobs; working-class women share the benefits of work, according to psychologists Sandra Scarr and Deborah Phillips of the University of Virginia and Kathleen McCartney of the University of New Hampshire. In reviewing 80 studies on this subject, they reported that working-class women with children say they would not leave work even if they didn't need the money. Work offers not only income but adult companionship, social contact and a connection with the wider world that they cannot get at home.

Looking at survey data from around the world, Scarr and Phillips wrote that the lives of mothers who work are not more stressful than the lives of those who are at home. So what about the second shift we've heard so much about? It certainly exists: in industrialized countries, researchers found, fathers work an average of 50 hours a week on the job and doing household chores; mothers work an average of 80 hours. Wethington and Kessler found that in daily "stress diaries" kept by husbands and wives, the women report more stress than the men do. But they also handle it better. In short, doing it all may be tough, but it doesn't wipe out the health benefits of working.

The Advantages for Families

What about the kids? Many working parents feel they want more time with their kids, and they say so. But does maternal employment harm children? In 1989 University of Michigan psychologist Lois Hoffman reviewed 50 years of research and found that the expected negative effects never materialized. Most often, children of employed and unemployed mothers didn't differ on measures of child development. But children of both sexes with working mothers have a less sex-stereotyped view of the world because fathers in two-income families tend to do more child care.

However, when mothers work, the quality of nonparental child care is a legitimate worry. Scarr, Phillips and McCartney say there is "near consensus among developmental psychologists and early-childhood experts that child care per se does not constitute a risk factor in children's lives." What causes problems, they report, is poor-quality care and a troubled family life. The need for good child care in this country has been obvious for some time.

What's more, children in two-job families generally don't lose out on one-to-one time with their parents. New studies, such as S. L. Nock and P. W. Kingston's *Time With Children: The Impact of Couples' Work-Time Commitments,* show that when both parents of preschoolers are working, they spend as much time in direct interaction with their children as families in which only the fathers work. The difference is that working parents spend more time with their kids on weekends. When only the husband works, parents spend more leisure time with each other. There is a cost to two-income families—the couples lose personal time—but the kids don't seem to pay it.

One question we never used to ask is whether having a working mother could be *good* for children. Hoffman, reflecting on the finding that employed women—both blue-collar and professional—register higher life-satisfaction scores than housewives, thinks it can be. She cites studies involving infants and older children, showing that a mother's satisfaction with her employment status relates positively both to "the quality of the mother-child interaction and to various indexes of the child's adjustment and abilities." For example, psychologists J. Guidubaldi and B. K. Nastasi of Kent State University reported in a 1987 paper that a mother's satisfaction with her job was a good predictor of her child's positive adjustment in school.

Again, this isn't true only for women in high-status jobs. In a 1982 study of sources of stress for children in low-income families, psychologists Cynthia Longfellow and Deborah Belle of the Harvard University School of Education found that employed women were generally less depressed than unemployed women. What's more, their children had fewer behavioral problems.

But the real point about working women and children is that work *isn't* the point at all. There are good mothers and not-so-good mothers, and some work and some don't. When a National Academy of Sciences panel reviewed the previous 50 years of research and dozens of studies in 1982, it found no consistent effects on children from a mother's working. Work is only one of many variables, the panel concluded in *Families That Work,* and not the definitive one.

What is the effect of women's working on their marriages? Having a working wife can increase psychological stress for men, especially older men, who grew up in a world where it was not normal for a wife to work. But men's expectations that they will—and must—be the only provider may be changing. Wethington and Kessler found that a wife's employment could be a significant buffer *against* depression for men born after 1945. Still, the picture of men's psychological well-being is very mixed, and class and expectations clearly play a role. Faludi cites polls showing that young blue-collar men are especially angry at women for invading what they see as their turf as breadwinners, even though a woman with such a job could help protect her husband from economic hardship. But in highly educated, dual-career couples, both partners say the wife's career has enhanced the marriage.

The First Shift: Women At Work

While women's own health and the well-being of their families aren't harmed by their working, what effect does this dual role have on their job performance? It's assumed that men can compartmentalize work and home lives but women will bring their home worries with them to work, making them distracted and inefficient employees.

The only spillover went in the other direction: The women brought their good feelings about their work home with them and left a bad day at home behind when they came to work. In fact, Wethington and Kessler found that it was the *men* who brought the family stresses with them to work. "Women are able to avoid bringing the contagion of home stress into the workplace," the researchers write, "whereas the inability of men to prevent this kind of contagion is pervasive." The researchers speculate that perhaps women get the message early on that they

can handle the home front, while men are taking on chores they
aren't trained for and didn't expect.

The Perils of Part-Time

Perhaps the most dangerous myth is that the solution to most
problems women suffer is for them to drop back—or drop out.
What studies actually show is a significant connection between a
reduced commitment to work and increased psychological stress.
In their Detroit study, Wethington and Kessler noted that women
who went from being full-time employees to full-time housewives
reported increased symptoms of distress, such as depression and
anxiety attacks; the longer a woman worked and the more committed she was to the job, the greater her risk for psychological
distress when she stopped.

What about part-time work, that oft-touted solution for weary
women? Women who work fewer than 20 hours per week, it turns
out, do not get the mental-health work benefit, probably because
they "operate under the fiction that they can retain full responsibility for child care and home maintenance," wrote Wethington
and Kessler. The result: Some part-timers wind up more stressed-
out than women working full-time. Part-time employment also
provides less money, fewer or no benefits and, often, less interesting work and a more arduous road to promotion.

That doesn't mean that a woman shouldn't cut down on her
work hours or arrange a more flexible schedule. But it does mean
she should be careful about jumping on a poorly designed mommy track that may make her a second-class citizen at work.

Many women think that when they have a baby, the best thing
for their mental health would be to stay home. Wrong once more.
According to Wethington and Kessler, having a baby does not
increase psychological distress for working women—*unless* the
birth results in their dropping out of the labor force. This doesn't
mean that any woman who stays home to care for a child is going
to be a wreck. But leaving the work force means opting out of the
benefits of being in it, and women should be aware of that.

As soon as a woman has any kind of difficulty—emotional,
family, medical—the knee-jerk reaction is to get her off the job.
No such solution is offered to men, despite the very real correla-
tion for men between job stress and heart attacks.

What the myth of the miserable working woman obscures is
the need to focus on how the *quality* of a woman's job affects her

health. Media stories warn of the alleged dangers of fast-track jobs. But our *Lifeprints* study found that married women in high-prestige jobs were highest in mental well-being; another study of life stress in women reported that married career women with children suffered the least from stress. Meanwhile, few media tears are shed for the women most at risk: those in the word-processing room who have no control at work, low pay and little support at home.

Women don't need help getting out of the work force; they need help staying in it. As long as much of the media continues to capitalize on national ignorance, that help will have to come from somewhere else. (Not that an occasional letter to the editor isn't useful.) Men need to recognize that they are not just occasional helpers but vital to the success of the family unit. The corporate culture has to be reshaped so that it doesn't run totally according to patterns set by the white male workaholic. This will be good for men *and* women. The government can guarantee parental leave and affordable, available child care. (It did so in the '40s, when women were needed in the factories.) Given that Congress couldn't even get a bill guaranteeing *unpaid* family leave passed last year [1991], this may take some doing. But hey, this is an election year.

II. SEXUAL HARASSMENT

EDITOR'S INTRODUCTION

Sexual harassment is not new. The Thomas-Hill hearings of 1991 served as a catalyst for discussion of some of the basic problems of male-female relations in the workplace: such as, what constitutes sexual harassment, should companies ban dating between coworkers, and how formally should men & women treat each other in the workplace. We are discovering that there is much unfinished business—the law provided women with the right to enter into male-dominated fields but it provided no road map for dealing with prejudice or anger once they got there. Sexual harassment is a symptom of confusion over changing roles and a lack of respect for the person who is being harassed. Many workers don't realize how new the laws are that protect individuals against sexual harassment. Women didn't start winning sexual harassment lawsuits until the mid-1970s. The first sexual harassment lawsuit to reach the Supreme Court was not decided until 1986.

Publications on sexual harassment and discrimination in this last year continually refer to the trauma of the Thomas-Hill hearings. "Judging Thomas," by Gloria Borger, captures the graphic nature of Professor Hill's testimony as well as the racially and sexually charged atmosphere that surrounded the nationally televised hearings. In the second article, "Sexual Harassment in the Workplace," Sheldon J. Stark gives a legal perspective on the hearings that answers some of the questions raised by the Thomas-Hill hearings. The third and fourth pieces highlight basic problems with the new sensitivity that swept the country in 1992. Written from the point of view of a small business owner, "Cultural Fascism" addresses the dark side of the improved legal remedies, asking if a sexual harassment lawsuit comes with a $300,000 price tag, then are women in the workplace being viewed as potentially dangerous liabilities? "The Grammar of Assent," by commentator William Buckley, addresses the costs of sexual harassment in human terms asking, 'Where has all the laughter gone?' The final article in this section, "The New Battle of the Sexes," takes a long range view of the causes of harassment, asserting that we are still not applying the same value system to men and women, nor are we treating each other with basic respect.

JUDGING THOMAS[1]

A painful public reunion with millions watching was not what anyone had planned: He, the self-made conservative Supreme Court nominee, defending his good name; she, the up-from-poverty legal scholar, accusing her former boss of "dirty" and "disgusting" behavior. Senate Judiciary Committee members were on trial, too, as members of a 98 percent male Senate club, accused of burying the accusations and being unable to understand the power of the charges of sexual harassment. It was a dirty circus, even by Washington standards. And when the public airing concluded, the stench lingered.

Never before had a nominee for the Supreme Court told the Senate it could take the job and shove it. "Confirm me if you want," Clarence Thomas declared defiantly. "Don't confirm me if you are so led." At first, he sounded almost ready to withdraw, but it was clear he was fighting mad. In a way, confirmation for the court became almost beside the point; Thomas's rage was directed at the system. In a righteous fury, he told his judges that their hearing was a "national disgrace. . . . You are ruining the country." He had been a victim, he said, of the vitriol of the left. His message: "Unless you kowtow to an old order . . . you will be lynched, destroyed, caricatured by a committee of the Senate rather than hung from a tree." The claims of his accuser, Anita Hill, were "unequivocally, uncategorically" wrong. He had not even watched her testimony.

Hill had given the most lurid description of any man's behavior that had ever been witnessed on network TV. The University of Oklahoma law professor told of a man who once pressed her for dates and then, when she refused, brought up sexual matters.

[1]Article by Gloria Borger. From *U.S. News & World Report* 111:33–36 O 21 '92. Copyright © Oct. 21, 1991 by U.S. News and World Report. Reprinted with permission.

"He talked about pornographic materials depicting individuals with large penises or large breasts involved in various sex acts," she said. "On other occasions, he referred to the size of his own penis as being larger than normal and he also spoke on some occasions of the pleasures he had given to women with oral sex." Her disgust was so great, she said, that she wound up in the hospital because of "stress on the job."

The nation was riveted by their testimony, and the host of witnesses for both sides. To some, Hill was Everywoman, the proxy for all who had ever had a degrading or threatening encounter with a male co-worker. To others, Thomas was the symbol of the devastation wrought by Washington's investigative machine run amok.

Someone had to be lying—or shading, or not remembering. Yet both witnesses seemed compelling in their own defense. Whatever the verdict, the fallout would be considerable: enlightening the rules of engagement between men and women; spreading the public's already mammoth disgust with government; forcing a re-examination of the confirmation process for high office. At the White House, aides quietly pondered future nominees to the court. And they debated whether the president would attack the Senate's handling of Thomas. In this, he would not be alone. "This is not advise and consent," an anguished Sen. John Danforth, Thomas's patron, told his colleagues. "This is slash and burn."

The Thomas affair is not just the story of one woman's testimony. It is the story of a system degraded by all its participants: the White House handlers trying to mute any discussion of the nominee's judicial philosophy, the congressional staffers searching for dirt, special interests looking to defeat the nomination to further their own causes. The administration's game plan was to make Thomas's triumphs over poverty and racism the key credentials. That left Thomas testifying that he had no opinion on almost everything, including *Roe v. Wade*. Character questions, always important, were the only way to strike at him. And it turned out that the biography that was to be his salvation included a chapter that could defeat him.

Nothing exposed the process to more disdain than the way the harassment allegations were unveiled. In late July [1991], the Alliance for Justice, an umbrella group of liberals leading the opposition to Thomas, received a phone call from a Yale Law School classmate of Anita Hill's who reported hearing that Hill

had complained of sexual harassment by Thomas while at the
Equal Employment Opportunity Commission. The group re-
ferred the matter to the staff of Sen. Howard Metzenbaum, an
Ohio Democrat and key Thomas opponent.

By September 3, Hill had been asked about the rumors but
did not disclose her own story. Meantime, the staff of Democrat
Edward Kennedy, another Thomas opponent, was doing its own
sleuthing. On September 5, Hill received a call from Labor subcommittee Kennedy staffer Ricki Seidman, who was interviewing
former EEOC employees on assorted issues and asked about reports of sexual harassment. Hill said she needed time to decide
whether she would respond.

Four days later, Seidman called back; Hill agreed to talk. In an
effort to raise the comfort level, Hill was referred to Metzenbaum
aide James Brudney, a law-school classmate. They spoke the next
day—and Hill outlined her charges against Thomas. Brudney,
who works for Metzenbaum on the Labor subcommittee, passed
the information along to Metzenbaum's staff on the Judiciary
Committee on September 11. Hill called the next day and spoke
with Harriet Grant, the committee's chief nominations counsel.

But there was a problem. Judiciary Committee Chairman Joseph Biden had made it clear he hoped questions about Thomas's
character were not to be the focus of his hearings. Some sources
say that even maverick Metzenbaum was concerned about crossing Biden on that point. And Kennedy would hardly be the prop-
er senator to raise an issue of sexual harassment—either publicly
or internally—given both his recent and ancient family problems.
Still, the conversations with Hill continued—often much to her
frustration. The point that stymied everything was her absolute
insistence that her charges be kept confidential.

The next days were full of misunderstandings. Hill thought
her September 12 request was simple: She wanted her charges
kept secret from Judge Thomas, yet made known to the committee. Her own political naiveté, sources say, led her to believe the
committee could consider her charges and, if they were found
credible, use them to prompt Thomas to withdraw quietly. In the
hot glare of national attention, Hill told the panel: "I made a
great effort to make sure it did not come to this."

But life in the Senate does not work that way: Grant, one of
several congressional-staff women who dealt with Hill, told the
professor that the committee's sense of fair play required that an
allegation against a nominee can be circulated to members only if
the nominee has a chance to respond. On September 18, the

committee was called by a corroborating witness. Two days later, Hill called—expecting members to be informed of her charges—and was once again told firmly that the committee's "hands are tied until we can confront the nominee."

Enter the FBI. By now, both sides were frustrated. An FBI investigation was suggested on September 21. Hill called the next day to reject the idea. On Sept. 23, she changed her mind and agreed to speak with the FBI—and to allow Thomas to be informed. Finally, after almost two weeks without any aggressive committee investigation, the process had begun. Hill sent a separate four-page personal statement to the committee. The same day, the White House was told of the charges.

Ken Duberstein, the former White House chief of staff retained as the official Thomas handler, wasted little time. He called Danforth, a longtime Thomas friend, to tell him the news—and Danforth called Thomas, who point-blank denied the allegations. The FBI report was rushed to completion in two days and amounted to a "she said, he said" back and forth that drew no conclusions about who was telling the truth. One additional witness corroborating Hill's story was also interviewed. The investigation was finished on September 25, just two days before the final committee vote.

That evening, Biden and ranking committee Republican Strom Thurmond took the report to Senate Majority Leader George Mitchell and Minority Leader Bob Dole. They decided to keep the matter quiet—to protect Hill's identity at her request. Biden spent the rest of the day and the entire next day informing his committee Democrats. Not a single member pushed for postponement or a closed-door session with Hill.

Once the story broke, Biden and his colleagues were skewered for their silence—and for the delay in investigating. "Would it not have been wise to call Anita Hill to meet with members of the committee?" asks Thomas supporter Republican Nancy Kassebaum, one of two women in the Senate. "As a group, they could have pointed out that if she continued to remain anonymous, her testimony would be invalid."

Biden was furious at the charges, saying it would have been "immoral" to force Hill to go public when she refused. "How can you have expected us to force Professor Hill, against her will, into the blinding light you see here today?" Biden explained at the outset of the hearings. "Events forced her to discuss these charges against her will."

Biden's greatest concern all along was leaks. When a senator on the committee was shown Hill's written statement, it was taken back. Members who chose to read the separate FBI report, like Paul Simon of Illinois, scanned it in the presence of a committee staffer and then returned it. Biden told Danforth at one point that he "wouldn't be surprised" if it all became public. The worry, says Danforth, was that "perhaps she would hold a press conference." As it turned out, he was worrying about the wrong leak.

The committee's vote was a cliffhanger—7 to 7—on September 27. But while the country was caught up in the public drama, the behind-the-scenes machinations over Anita Hill were just as compelling: When he heard of the allegations, Simon was disturbed enough to call Hill himself. She asked that he distribute copies of her statement about Thomas to all members of the Senate, while keeping her name anonymous; he explained it was "impossible" and tried to persuade her to testify. When he failed, Simon still sought no delay in the committee vote. Fellow Democrat Patrick Leahy did not read the "For Senators Only" envelope containing Hill's statement until the day of the vote. "We all wanted to know whether there was any way to get this woman to testify," he says. "This should have come out in the hearings—and there's no way we can do that over."

If Republicans seemed more sanguine, it was because many remained uninformed. Thurmond now says "they could have all read the FBI report," but some now complain they never knew one existed. Charles Grassley of Iowa says he only learned of the news "while we were sitting there the day of the final vote." In passing, a colleague asked, "Did you hear the latest?" Grassley had not. Thurmond did tell Hatch and Arlen Specter of Pennsylvania. Hatch called Thomas, who denied the charges: "I don't know why she would make a comment like that." Specter called Danforth and then asked Thomas about the allegations in his office the day of the vote. But Republican Hank Brown of Colorado was told by GOP staff there was "nothing significant" in the charges. When he later read the FBI report after the news became public, he considered it significant enough to call Hill herself. The language in the report, she told him, was not as explicit as the actual comments. At the hearing, Hill filled in the missing details.

Hours before the full Senate was scheduled to vote on Thomas, there was still no clear inclination to delay the vote. It took a national uproar and unusual pressure in the Capitol to change the dynamic. Women from the House marched across the

Capitol to demand a hearing from their male Senate colleagues. Congressional switchboards were jammed. In a private Republican caucus, Kassebaum told her male colleagues that "it is important for Clarence Thomas to take the initiative and try to clear his name." He had not done so because his handlers were still being assured by some Democrats that things were not yet out of control. But the Democratic leaders misjudged their own flock, and the public. Finally, the numbers dictated the outcome: Enough Democrats were defecting to insure a loss for Thomas. And so plans were made for a full airing of Hill's charges before the Judiciary Committee and a Senate vote on the nomination this week.

In fact, the 10-year-old case Hill presented was hardly ideal, raising serious questions of credibility. Why did Hill, a lawyer dedicated to rooting out harassment who worked in the very agency charged with defending women's rights, never file a complaint against Thomas? Why, if she felt harassed, had she switched jobs to continue to work with him when he moved from the Education Department to the EEOC in 1982? She explained she was young, and vulnerable, and worried about raising a charge that could cost her her job. "I'm embarrassed I didn't say anything," she said. And she further explained the harassment had stopped for a while, leading her to believe that following him to the EEOC would be all right. She did not dispute phone logs showing that she kept in touch with Thomas in the years since she left Washington, but the contention of Thomas defenders that they were evidence of a cordial relationship, she said, was "garbage." Still, Hill said when all was done that she would not have aired the charge at all had she not been approached by committee staffers.

At the end of the most extraordinary television showdown, it was Clarence Thomas's ringing condemnation of the process that struck the most powerful note. This was the real nominee speaking. "From the very beginning, charges were leveled against me from the shadows, charges of drug abuse, antisemitism, wife beating, drug use by family members," he said. "This is not American, this is Kafkaesque. It has got to stop. It must stop for the benefit of future nominees and our country."

In the middle of the storm last week, Danforth went to visit Thomas at home. He offered comfort, telling his friend he was sorry. "And it wasn't an expression of pity. I meant I'm sorry for what I've done." Never again, says Danforth, would he advise anybody to take a job that requires confirmation by the United States Senate. As Thomas himself told his judges, "No job is worth what I have been through." If Thomas withdraws his name altogether—or the Senate ultimately votes him down—the court vacancy still will need filling. But by whom? Danforth's prediction: "All of our nominees are going to be people who come from the mountains of New Hampshire—or suckers."

SEXUAL HARASSMENT IN THE WORKPLACE: LESSONS FROM THE THOMAS-HILL HEARINGS[2]

Political satirist Mark Russell suggests that the Clarence Thomas-Anita Hill hearings were not a total loss. As a result of the hearings, he says, October 1991 became National Sexual Harassment Awareness Month. Perhaps. The problem for lawyers concerned about a woman's right to be free from sexual oppression in the workplace is whether that awareness has been a plus or a minus. What lessons were learned by the millions of people who sat glued to their television sets? Did the hearings advance the struggle against sexual harassment in the workplace or cause a retreat?

On the one hand, we learned that sexual harassment is pervasive, that it occurs in all social and economic classes, and that no woman is immune. Astute observers may even have learned that sexual harassment is about power, not sex. We also learned how difficult it is to prove charges of sexual harassment against high-level officials and wrongdoers.

Perhaps more significant, we learned something most lawyers already knew: how easy it is to discredit the victim. Indeed, on display in the Thomas-Hill hearings was the defense strategy most often resorted to in discrimination cases—it's called "plaintiff-bashing." And if Anita Hill, a bright, accomplished, and articulate law professor—in fact, a person of conservative politi-

[2]Article by Sheldon J. Stark, vice-chair of the Employment Rights Advisory Committee of the American Trial Lawyer's Association. From *Trial* 28(5):166–122 My '92. Copyright © May, 1992 by The Association of Trial Lawyers of America. Reprinted with permission of *Trial*.

cal values who had backed the Robert Bork nomination to the Supreme Court—could be so thoroughly vilified, what ordinary woman would stand a chance of being believed?

Some women, no doubt, were positively affected by what they saw and will now have the courage to come forward. They learned that they are not alone, that there are others out there with similar experiences. Indeed, some of my colleagues in the management defense bar report an increase in the number of sexual harassment filings in the months since the hearings.

Other women will draw a different lesson. They now understand what it means to face hostile cross-examination. For them, new demons have surfaced, bringing dread and apprehension as to the kind of "dirt" the company might dig up about them. These women will be unwilling to run the risk of seeking redress.

Persistent Confusion

Even after the hearings, it is surprising how uninformed most people remain about just what sexual harassment is, what is or is not illegal, and just what a victim can do about it. Why was there so much ambiguity and confusion? Why does it persist? Why did the media do such a poor job of explaining it to the public?

The problem, I submit, is that the law of sexual harassment is still in its infancy, and its interpretation and enforcement remain heavily politicized. Probably the first national law prohibiting discrimination against women came with passage of the Equal Pay Act, which made it illegal to pay men and women different wages for performing the same work.

The act did not become law until 1961. That is recent history. Sex discrimination in general did not become illegal until July 1, 1965, when Title VII became effective. Title VII did not prohibit discrimination against government employees like Anita Hill until 1972.

Ironically, the sex discrimination provisions were added to Title VII at the last minute by *opponents* of the bill who were trying to defeat Title VII's anti-race-discrimination provisions. Southern conservatives and their allies thought that the addition of laws against sex discrimination would effectively convert the bill into a joke they could then laugh to death.

Joseph Rauh, a Washington civil rights lawyer who was involved in the Title VII negotiations, credits then-Michigan Rep. Martha Griffiths with convincing a reluctant congressional lead-

ership that sex discrimination was not a joke, that the Equal Pay
Act had not solved all problems women faced in the workplace,
and that the amendments offered by the conservatives adding sex
discrimination to the bill should be accepted.

Only Yesterday

In Michigan, where I practice, sex discrimination prohibi-
tions were not added to the Michigan Fair Employment Practices
Act until 1965, a full 10 years after race, national origin, and
religious discrimination were made illegal in the workplace. Due
to constitutional challenges from employers, however, the sex discrimination amendments did not become effective until 1967.

Anyone who might be tempted to view this as long ago and far
away should remember a 1972 interview with Prime Minister
Chou En-lai of China. When asked for his thoughts on the impact
of the French Revolution of 1789, the Prime Minister replied,
"It's too soon to tell." In a profession that still has to deal with the
rule against perpetuities, the rule in Shelley's case, and the statute
of frauds, the civil rights acts can be said to have been passed only
yesterday.

From the outset, there was little or no confusion concerning
the intent of the laws against sex discrimination. Sexual harassment, however, was another matter. The first reported case of
sexual harassment under Title VII was not decided until 1974, 10
years after the law's 1964 passage and only 6 years before Anita
Hill's alleged problems with Clarence Thomas began. Believe it or
not, the decision in the first—and to date the only—case of sexual
harassment ever decided by the U.S. Supreme Court—*Meritor
Savings Bank, FSB v. Vinson*—was issued in 1986, twenty-two years
after passage of Title VII.

Meritor Savings Bank was a unanimous decision written by
Chief Justice William Rehnquist. He put to rest a controversy
many lawyers, and most of the public, didn't even know existed:
"Without question, when a supervisor sexually harasses a subordinate because of the subordinate's sex, that supervisor discriminates on the basis of sex."

The earliest cases did *not* accept the proposition that sexual
advances by a supervisor toward a subordinate constituted discrimination on the basis of sex. Indeed, the first claims were
thrown out of court. How, these courts asked, is seeking sexual
favors from an attractive woman discrimination because of sex?

In *Barnes v. Costle,* however, the district court's rejection of the plaintiff's sexual harassment claims was reversed. The District of Columbia Federal Court of Appeals developed an enterprising approach to fit sexual harassment cases into Title VII's prohibition against discrimination "because of sex."

The court noted that the supervisor in the case made unwelcome sexual advances exclusively to female employees. Therefore, the women were targeted "because of sex" and the employer was liable. Of course, if the supervisor in *Barnes* had been bisexual, seeking favors equally from men and women, even the D.C. Court of Appeals might not have been able to find liability under Title VII. Obviously, the courts were struggling to find a way to remedy a wrong, and the early efforts were halting and strained.

For example, the first time sexual harassment appeared in Michigan state court was in a 1977 case, *Tash v. Houston.* A lawyer using computerized research tools like *WESTLAW* or *LEXIS* would not find *Tash* under "sexual harassment." Not only did the plaintiff not base her claim on the state civil rights statute, but she didn't even use the words "sexual harassment."

Tash was secretary to a union local president. She was discharged, she alleged, when she refused his sexual advances. Sexual harassment theories were so new, untried, and risky that her attorney found a remedy in the common law. He resorted to the somewhat exotic liability theory of tortious interference with contract.

What Took Her So Long?

This, then, was the climate of legal and judicial opinion in 1981. Yet certain senators wondered, in October 1991, why Anita Hill had not complained at the time she was allegedly experiencing sexual harassment in her place of work. According to the polls, this charge—that her complaints weren't timely—became one of the most devastating blows to her credibility in the public mind. (Significantly, that charge did not bother the judiciary. A *National Law Journal* poll revealed that a substantial majority of state judges believed Hill over Thomas, the reverse of the public's response.)

In talking with lay groups about sexual harassment after the hearings, I found that Hill's delay in coming forward seemed to bother people the most. Yet had Title VII's limitations been explained early on in the hearings, this charge could very well have been laid to rest.

When Anita Hill worked for the Department of Education's Office of Civil Rights and later for the Equal Employment Opportunity Commission (EEOC), she was, of course, a federal employee. For federal employees, Title VII has been virtually the only law protecting women from sexual harassment and sex discrimination. Title VII would probably have been her exclusive remedy. In 1981, when she could have brought her charge on a timely basis, she faced three major obstacles.

First, Thomas was the person in charge at the Office of Civil Rights and later at the EEOC—the nation's chief law-enforcement officer for discrimination and sexual harassment. Filing a Title VII charge under these circumstances would have been like asking a fox to investigate his own raid on the chicken coop.

Second, Hill's charges would have been tantamount to an accusation that Thomas wanted to "ride with the cops and cheer for the robbers." Thomas was a political appointee, and his sponsors probably would have defended his reputation, which reflected on them, by attacking Hill's character. This response to her charges would likely have been immediate and intense. For a young, black, female lawyer who had struggled out of poverty, the travail would have been almost unbearable, the career damage irreversible. In 1991, her credentials were insufficient to protect her. In 1981, when her résumé still had few entries, she would have been devoured.

Third, if Anita Hill *had* attempted to file charges of sexual harassment, there would have been no remedy available to her. From its passage, Title VII was armed only with equitable remedies: back pay, reinstatement, injunctive relief, and attorney fees. Since Hill had lost neither her job nor any salary she was not entitled to back pay and had no need for reinstatement. Her salary and health insurance undoubtedly covered the five days she spent in the hospital suffering from stomach pains and stress, so she had no economic losses.

As to injunctive relief, the charges would have been vigorously denied. As noted, in 1981 Hill would have had substantially less credibility than she had in the hearings. She was then a young lawyer with virtually no experience. Thomas was one of the highest black officials in the federal government. What federal judge would have issued an injunction under such circumstances? Even had Hill prevailed, the only compensation that might have been awarded—attorney fees—would have gone to her lawyer, not to her. What rational person would have risked everything for so limited a return? Is it any wonder that no charges were filed?

The Civil Rights Act of 1991, approved by Congress on November 7, 1991, now makes compensatory and punitive damages available for claims brought under Title VII. The act also gives government employees the right to jury trials in these cases but excludes them from the new punitive damages provisions.

As a result, Hill would now be able to claim emotional distress damages. These are notoriously hard to prove, and the new Civil Rights Act has not changed the climate of opinion, public and judicial, in which such charges would necessarily be received. So although she would be somewhat better off under today's law than she was 10 years ago, her remedies would still be limited.

Interestingly, in the months since the hearings, the issue has not gone away. The public thirsts for more information about sex harassment. Since the hearings, many bar associations, universities, and women's groups have sponsored seminars on the topic.

Sex and Power

There should be no mystery about what is and is not sexual harassment. In 1980, the EEOC issued guidelines defining it. Under the regulations, sexual harassment comes in three basic forms: (1) quid pro quo, (2) retaliation, and (3) hostile environment.

Quid pro quo, Latin for "what for what," is the classic form of sexual harassment. "Sleep with me and I'll give you the promotion." "Be nice to me and I'll be nice to you." Clearly, such demands are more about power than sex.

Retaliation claims are equally clear and well understood. "So you won't sleep with me? You're fired!" "Reject my advances? I'm giving the supervisor's job to someone else." More commonly, retaliation and reprisal take the form of increasing pressure on and isolation of the victim. The rejected superior gives poor performance reviews and takes other actions designed to make the victim fail or leave voluntarily. Again, it is clearly the exercise of power rather than sex that is at the heart of the matter.

Recently, most litigation in these cases has been in the area of "hostile environment." When does the workplace become polluted enough with sexual comments, nude pictures, and humiliating horseplay to become actionable?

Federal regulations define a hostile environment as one with "unwelcome sexual advances, requests for sexual favors, and other verbal or physical conduct of a sexual nature . . . when . . . such conduct has the purpose or effect of unreasonably interfering with an individual's work performance or creating an intimidating, hostile, or offensive working environment."

The conceptual problem for the courts and the public comes from distinguishing unlawful sexual harassment from the enjoyable, innocent flirting that often makes it fun to go to work. Moreover, many people meet their future spouses where they work. Do the sexual harassment laws make it too dangerous to risk seeking a date at the office or the shop?

In *Tomkins v. Public Service Electric & Gas Co.*, the district court said, "If the plaintiff's view were to prevail, no superior could, prudently, attempt to open a social dialogue with any subordinate of either sex. An invitation to dinner could become an invitation to a federal lawsuit if a once harmonious relationship turns sour at some later time."

Federal law and most states' statutes, including Michigan's, attempt to draw a "bright line" between acceptable, even pleasant, behavior on the one hand, and illegal, oppressive behavior on the other. That bright line springs from the word "unwelcome," which appears in federal regulations and state statutes.

In *Meritor Savings Bank,* the court was careful to distinguish between voluntary or involuntary on the one hand, and welcome or unwelcome on the other. According to the Supreme Court, "the fact that sex-related conduct was 'voluntary,' in the sense that the complainant was not forced to participate against her will, is not a defense to a sexual harassment suit brought under Title VII. . . . The correct inquiry is whether [the victim] by her conduct indicated that the alleged sexual advances were unwelcome, not whether her actual participation in sexual intercourse was voluntary."

According to the EEOC Policy Guidelines on Sexual Harassment, the agency has approved this definition: "The challenged conduct must be unwelcome 'in the sense that the employee did not solicit or incite it, and in the sense that the employee regarded the conduct as undesirable or offensive.'"

Without saying so expressly, the courts and the EEOC seem to have moved sexual harassment law into line with the old "dog bite" rule (under which every dog got one bite). A person can't know if a colleague or subordinate regards sexual overtures as undesirable or offensive before trying and being rejected.

Where the subordinate was too frightened to say "no" to her boss, there is probably some ambiguity as to whether he understood that the offensive conduct was unwelcome. Under *Meritor Savings Bank,* however, the risk of liability is rightly borne by the employer whose manager took a chance and made the offensive advances. In my experience, this ambiguity is generally a jury question, and the case law has not been troubled deeply by the distinction.

The major controversies of late have been in two areas.

• Whose viewpoint should be used to evaluate the offensiveness of a hostile environment, that of a reasonable person (generally meaning a man) or that of a reasonable woman? Men and women may have significantly different attitudes on this subject, and selecting the test or viewpoint by which to judge will most often determine the outcome. Employers have argued for the former and victims for the latter.

• Employer representatives in recent cases have sought to undermine the purpose of Title VII in the sexual-harassment context by arguing that the law wasn't meant to change existing conditions. If the environment was sexually polluted before plaintiff entered it, they say, there should be no liability.

In the *Rabidue v. Osceola Refining Co.* case, for example, both issues were before the appellate court. The majority came down hard on the side of the employer. The court quoted the district judge with approval:

Indeed, it cannot seriously be disputed that in some work environments, humor and language are rough hewn and vulgar. Sexual jokes, sexual conversations and girlie magazines may abound. Title VII was not meant to—or can—change this. It must never be forgotten that Title VII is the federal court mainstay in the struggle for equal employment opportunity for the female workers of America. But it is quite different to claim that Title VII was designed to bring about a magical transformation in the social mores of American workers.

According to the Sixth Circuit, therefore, if the environment was sexually hostile before the plaintiff entered it, there could be no liability to her for sexual harassment unless there was an increase in its level after she took the job.

The court also came out squarely in favor of the reasonable-person standard: "The trier of fact, when judging the totality of the circumstances impacting upon the asserted abusive and hostile environment placed in issue by the plaintiff's charges, must adopt the perspective of a reasonable person's reaction to a similar environment under essentially like or similar circumstances."

Indeed, returning to the "good old days" of the earliest sexual harassment decisions, the Sixth Circuit chose to reject any approach that found liability where males and females were equally mistreated: "It is of significance to note that instances of complained of sexual conduct that prove equally offensive to male and female workers would not support a Title VII sexual harassment charge because both men and women were accorded like treatment."

A number of circuits have been very critical of *Rabidue*. Fortunately, the Sixth Circuit has retreated from these antiquated and unsympathetic attitudes. It has restored, for example, a gender-conscious standard that requires that the conduct be viewed from the victim's perspective.

The reaction of the courts in my state to the kind of arguments so well received in *Rabidue* demonstrates why most lawyers in Michigan litigate under state rather than federal law and are likely to continue to do so even though the Civil Rights Act of 1991 has gone into effect. In *Radtke v. Everett,* the Michigan Court of Appeals, emphatically rejecting the *Rabidue* approach, wrote an opinion that makes lawyers who represent sexual harassment victims proud to be participating in this kind of litigation:

We believe that the adoption of the reasonable person standard, coupled with the consideration of the level of "obscenity" that pervaded the workplace before and after plaintiff's arrival, strips the provisions of the state Civil Rights Act of their effect. In essence, the principles in *Rabidue* prevent the state Civil Rights Act from achieving its purpose of eliminating sexual harassment from the workplace and ensuring employees the right to work in an environment free from discriminatory intimidation, ridicule, and insult.

Accordingly, we adopt the "reasonable woman" perspective. This standard, which ensures a gender-conscious review of sexual harassment, will help enable women to participate in the workforce on an equal footing with men, and prevent the trivializing of the effects of sexual harassment that has previously occurred under the gender-neutral "reasonable person" standard.

Judge Harold Hood, who wrote *Radtke,* was inducted into the Michigan Women's Hall of Fame in part because of this opinion. The employer in *Radtke* is seeking review by Michigan's supreme court.

The struggle, of course, is far from over. The law has a great deal of maturing to do. Without putting too fine a point on it, every one of these cases ultimately becomes a mixed question of fact and law. Because resolution of these issues ultimately is political, pro-business federal judges appointed by conservative Republican presidents seem likely to continue to create a hostile environment for discrimination cases in federal court for the foreseeable future. Presidents Reagan and Bush have now appointed more than half the federal judges in the country. No wonder employment lawyers often feel that the decisions seem to be moving backward rather than forward.

Ultimately, the lessons taught by the Thomas-Hill hearings will be learned differently in different parts of the country and by different segments of our society. We can only hope that whatever lessons are learned will advance the cause of equal rights in the workplace.

CULTURAL FASCISM[3]

On the same day that Ted Kennedy asked forgiveness for his personal "shortcomings," he advocated slapping lottery-size punitive damages on small-business owners who may be guilty of excessive flirting, or whose employees may be guilty of talking dirty. Senator Kennedy expressed regrets that the new civil rights bill caps punitive damages for sexual harassment as high as $300,000 (depending on company size), and he promises to push for increases next year. Note that the senators have voted to exempt themselves from punitive damages.

I am the owner of a small restaurant/bar that employs approximately 20 young males whose role models range from Axl Rose to John Belushi. They work hard in a high-stress, fast-paced job in a hot kitchen and at times they are guilty of colorful language. They have also been overheard telling Pee-wee Herman jokes and listening to obnoxious rock lyrics. They have discussed pornography and they have flirted with waitresses. One chef/manager has asked out a pretty blonde waitress probably 100 times in three years. She seems to enjoy the game, but always

[3]Article by Sarah J. McCarthy. From *Forbes* 148:116 D 9 '91. Copyright © 1991 by Forbes, Inc. Reprinted with permission.

says no. Everyone calls everyone else "Honey"—it's a ritual, a way of softening what sound like barked orders; "I need the medium-rare shish kebab *now!*"

"Honey" doesn't mean the same thing here as it does in women's studies departments or at the EEOC. The auto body shop down the street has pinups. Perhaps under the vigilant eyes of the feminist political correctness gestapo we can reshape our employees' behavior so they act more like nerds from the Yale women's studies department. The gestapo will not lack for potential informers seeking punitive damages and instant riches.

With the Civil Rights Bill of 1991 we are witnessing the most organized and systematic assault on free speech and privacy since the McCarthy era. The vagueness of the sexual harassment law, combined with our current litigation explosion, is a frightening prospect for small businesses. We are now financially responsible for sexually offensive verbal behavior, even if we don't know it is occurring, under a law that provides no guidelines to define "offensive" and "harassment." This is a cultural fascism unmatched since the Chinese communists outlawed hand-holding, decorative clothing and premarital sex.

This law is detrimental even to the women it professes to help. I am a feminist, but the law has made me fearful of hiring women. If one of our cooks or managers—or my husband or sons—offends someone, it could cost us $100,000 in punitive damages and legal expenses. There will be no insurance fund or stockholders or taxpayers to pick up the tab.

When I was a feminist activist in the Seventies, we knew the dangers of a pedestal—it was said to be as confining as any other small place. As we were revolted and outraged by the woman-hatred in violent pornography, we reminded each other that education, not laws, was the solution to our problems. In *Women Against Sexist Violence in Pornography and Media* in Pittsburgh, we were well aware of the dangers of encroaching on the First Amendment. Free speech was, perhaps more than anything else, what made our country grow into a land of enlightenment and diversity. The lesbians among us were aware that the same laws used to censor pornography could be used against them if their sexual expressions were deemed offensive.

We admired powerful women writers such as Marge Piercy and poets like Robin Morgan who swooped in from nowhere, writing break-your-chains poems about women swinging from crystal chandeliers like monkey vines and defecating in punch bowls. Are we allowed to talk about these poems in the current American workplace?

The lawyers—the prim women and men who went to the politically correct law schools—believe with sophomoric arrogance that the solution to all the world's problems is tort litigation. We now have eternally complicated questions of sexual politics judged by the shifting standards of the reasonable prude.

To the leadership of the women's movement: You do women a disservice. You ladies—and I use that term intentionally—have trivialized the women's movement. You have made us ladies again. You have not considered the unintended effects of your sexual harrassment law. You are saying that too many things men say and do with each other are too rough-and-tumble for us. Wielding the power of your $300,000 lawsuits, you are frightening managers into hiring men over women. I know that I am so frightened. You have installed a double pane of glass on the glass ceiling with the help of your white knight and protector, Senator Kennedy.

You and your allies tried to lynch Clarence Thomas. You alienate your natural allies. Men and women who wanted to work shoulder to shoulder with you are now looking over their shoulders. You have made women into china dolls that if broken come with a $300,000 price tag. The games, intrigue, nuances and fun of flirting have been made into criminal activity.

We women are not as delicate and powerless as you think. We do not want victim status in the workplace. Don't try to foist it on us.

THE GRAMMAR OF ASSENT[4]

I have to confess that ever since Anita Hill happened I have been waiting, along with, I'd guess, ten million other males, for someone to write or say something about male–female banter that would restore a little perspective to the social scene. I'd have done it myself, except that it really did need to come from a woman to be entirely credible, and so we waited, for months . . . what seemed like years. And then on Friday, David

[4]Article by William F. Buckley, Jr. From *National Review* 45:62 J 18 '92. Copyright © 1992 by National Review, Inc. Reprinted with permission.

Margolick of the *New York Times* wrote about Judge Maryanne
Barry of the Federal District Court in New Jersey, the crowning
line of whose speech delivered to nine hundred federal law-
enforcement agents and officials in Washington was, "Where has
the laughter gone?"

The disclaimers are both necessary and sincere. They are that
most men vigorously oppose sexual "harassment" (as does Judge
Barry). There is no question about it that if Anita Hill was telling
the exact truth, she was indeed "harassed" by Clarence Thomas
when he was her superior in the Equal Employment Opportunity
Commission.

But what happened as a result of the charges by Miss Hill was
a metamorphosis in the meaning of the word "harassment" of a
kind that threatened to alter the nature of heterosexual relations.
Judge Barry was on the point. Because of a few "professional
hypochondriacs," she said:

good and well-meaning men are afraid to be themselves, and the more
serious problems women face in the work force remain unaddressed. . . .
What is happening is that every sexy joke of long ago, every flirtation, is
being recalled by some women and revised and re-evaluated as sexual
harassment. Many of these accusations are, in anybody's book, frivolous.
Frivolous accusations reduce, if not eliminate, not only communication
between men and women but any kind of playfulness and banter.

One has to begin at the beginning, as though one were an
androgynous Martian visiting the planet Earth for the first time
and asking such questions as, How do men and women get to
know each other well enough to make dates, let alone to agree to
contract marriage? The kindergarten-Martian teacher would
have to say something on the order of, "Well, the tradition is for
the male to approach the female, rather than vice versa. And
depending on the culture, the approach follows any of several
lines. In some cultures, in some ages, introductions were made
only by parents or guardians, and all joint activities were super-
vised. But in many modern cultures, the young men and the
young women are left pretty much on their own, but still the
convention is for the male to make the advances."

If asked just how such advances are made, the teacher would
need to explain, "Well, it depends a great deal on the stylistic
disposition of the man/boy who of course would be aware of the
stylistic pre-inclinations of the woman/girl he was addressing. In
some cases, flowers would be sent, with a little note. In days gone
by, such notes were very often very formal. [I know of an ardent

suitor in the Twenties who sent his equivalent of love-letters to his inamorata, signed, Yrs., Chas.] But these days," the teacher would go on, "there is a high degree of informality. Sometimes the ice is broken by the telling of off-color stories, usually by the man to the woman, but often the other way around. And . . . one thing leads to another, and eventually there is a scene at the altar, at which these days about 50 per cent of the brides are actually pregnant."

Judge Barry was hardly endorsing Haight-Ashbury style effronteries. She related how she felt stung by the tongue-lashing one female lawyer gave her for calling a young woman a "girl." How would young women today treat it if the judge referred to them, informally, as girls? "Some visibly coil up like cobras, narrow their eyes and their mouths, and spit out some answer which usually includes the word, 'shocked.'"

Anybody surveying that article on Friday was confident that not more than a week would pass before Judge Barry was attacked by the Women's Pre-emptive Rights League. They'd have been right. The *New York Times*' Anna Quindlen fired at her 48 hours later, "I'm disappointed that Judge Barry perpetuated the nutty anti-feminist myth that the world is full of overbearing women who go berserk if you send them roses." But I bet if I sent roses tomorrow to Miss Quindlen she would be offended. It is really amazing what Romeo got away with in pursuing Juliet.

THE *NEW* BATTLE OF THE SEXES[5]

Now that the dust has cleared a bit and we've gone through the knee-jerk reaction to Clarence Thomas-Anita Hill and the whole issue of sexual harassment, maybe we are clearheaded enough to take on the real bottom-line cause of the issue—the basic undeniable differences in the way men and women *think*.

Body parts aside, and immature macho egotism notwithstanding, there has not been any real improvement in efforts to decipher why men and women never really understand one another—on the sexual-harassment issue or on *any* issue.

Many of the national editorials, the talk-show discussions, and

[5]Article by Gerry T. Fulcher. From *Industry Week* 241/9:22–26 My 4 '92. Copyright © 1992 by Penton Publishing, Inc., Cleveland, OH. Reprinted with permission.

even the heated debates of the lunatic fringes on both sides have dissected virtually every aspect of the actions and the words that constitute harassment, sexual or otherwise. But none has asked the real question: What explains the attitude-development process of men that has resulted in a general belittling of female ability and, therefore, has given men a self-proclaimed right to put women down? According to most experts in the field of human relations, the actions and words of harassment will change only if attitudes change.

In recent months we have had a few examples that make this point clear.

Magic Johnson, millionaire athlete extraordinaire, elicited international shock and then sympathy when he announced he had tested HIV positive. Many of us, especially most of us men, were so busy giving him standing ovations and sympathetically expressing our sorrow that we never bothered to look at the underlying cause of his physical ailment. He had been living a dissolute, irresponsible, free-wheeling, self-gratifying lifestyle of meaningless sexual encounters with just about any woman who came his way for a period of years. You can be absolutely certain that if a female athlete came forward with an announcement about getting AIDS because she had slept with hundreds and hundreds and hundreds of men, the national reaction would have been quite different. The very first reaction of society in general, and of men in particular, would have been, "What a slut. She got what she deserved for all that promiscuity."

Is there any one of us under the height of seven feet who would dare to say of Magic Johnson, "He played sexual Russian roulette and got what he deserved for being irresponsible?"

What all of this means when we consider the sexual-harassment issue is that only after we apply the same value system to both men and women when considering their worth and their behavior will we understand the root cause of harassment and discrimination. This issue is not a made-for-TV news conference or an explosive Congressional hearing in the mold of a *National Enquirer* expose. If we are honest, we will admit that these kinds of inequities exist every day in virtually every workplace setting throughout the country. The more honest among us will have to admit that these kinds of value judgments are being made every day. It comes from that basic mistrust and the suspicions that many men harbor about women who have invaded what they consider to be male turf—the workplace.

No pervasive mindset could possibly exist without a long-documented conditioning process. And the conditioning process that "permits" men to believe that women are inferior goes as far back as Aristotle in 350 B.C., when he put it bluntly: "The man is superior to the female. The one rules, and the other is to be ruled. The real glory of man is shown by commanding, and the glory of the woman is in obeying." This theme has even received inspirational support from the likes of St. Paul: "Man was not created for the woman, but woman was created for the man."

In the 1800s, Nietzsche added fuel to the discrimination fire with his views on the "place" of women: "Men shall be trained for the war, and women trained for the recreation of the men." His views, which are still taught in colleges today, are imitated and often paraphrased in half the employee lounges in the U.S.

From the other side of the issue, women also have undergone a rigid conditioning, to which many of them have succumbed—namely, that they are to accept the male mentality about staying in one's "place." After all, women were denied the right to vote until 1920, a mere first step toward equality. History teaches over and over that a single act of equality does not produce an *attitude* of equality (at least not in one generation).

What has become obvious is that women's attitudes have changed as quickly as our progress in the field of aviation. We have gone from the Wright brothers' 100-ft flight in 1903 to out-of-space forays, all in less than a century. It is becoming obvious that the last decade of this century is going to result in more progress in the equality of women, whether men like it or not. Unfortunately, many men will not surrender unconditionally.

During the last few months there has been ample hand-wringing and group apologies for blatant insensitivities, some reforms about language at the water cooler, and a lot fewer close encounters at Xerox machines. But little has been said or done about the real issue: basic respect. A lot more men may be watching their workplace behavior, but there is little evidence that there are any heartfelt changes in attitudes. Some women say that the remarks that used to be spoken loudly are now merely whispered. A CBS/*New York Times* poll recently showed that 40% of women say that sexual harassment is still going on, and as many as 50% of men admit to performing acts that could definitely be considered to be sexually harassing.

Poll after poll indicates that the complaints of sexual harass-ment will increase significantly, and, yes, there may even be a moderate increase in false accusations. The reality is that the entire matter will eventually be resolved only after a significant effort by employers to stress the importance on the underlying causes and not merely on establishing new rules for "acceptable behavior." The real problem lies in the reality that there is no identifiable means of measuring the thinking process involved.

Many men may not like to hear the findings of one study that indicates that it's going to take another few years for real change, and that real change will take place abruptly as more females become bosses. For now, don't expect too much real reform.

A recent study showed that men *don't* think it's inappropriate to compliment specific body parts of females, because those same men say *they* would be highly flattered if women were to praise the male body parts. It's clear we all still have a long way to go.

Why do so many women seem to still just "take it"? The Clarence Thomas-Anita Hill hearings did result in some valuable lessons. First of all, the hearings demonstrated that if men in general don't understand this subject to some degree, male members of the Judiciary Committee don't understand it at all. Government is supposed to be representative of the attitudes of society. On this subject it was obvious that Congress is about 20 years behind the times.

There is additional evidence of ignorance in that Congress passed a law some time ago protecting its members from complaints of employees who are harassed. If the term "You just don't get it" ever had any meaning, that is it.

One of the most ignorant of all comments about Ms. Hill's position was made by one of the intellectual giants on the committee who said, "If all of this is true, how come you just 'took it' without doing anything about it?" Even those who support Ms. Hill's position have neglected the most basic reason of all: Women in general are simply more patient, more understanding, more considerate, and more forgiving than men are and, unfortunately, more used to being victimized.

While people try to imagine the answers, it's clear that the truth lies in some documented statistics. Mental-health professionals and addiction therapists, for instance, have established that nine out of 10 women in relationships with alcoholic partners will stay with the drinker in order to help, but that nine out of 10 men in relationships with alcoholic women will leave them. What does that tell us about who takes suffering better? Most of us more honest men will admit that the women in our lives have accepted and forgiven us for things that we could have never accepted and forgiven them for.

The primary responsibility for initiating improvement on this particular issue lies squarely with the man. It is the man who will have to improve his attitude and his behavior. We will have to reform our collective immaturity regarding women as co-workers. Women are not there for our diversion, our relaxation, or as the butt of our sexist jokes—and certainly not for the more serious harassment.

One of the realities that men must accept is that, given the right opportunity, there is not a single piece of objective evidence that indicates women cannot do virtually every job just as well as men can. And, if there *are* differences in the level of job performance, it has nothing to do with gender. Preconceived prejudices aside, women are not inferior workers, and it is a miscarriage of justice that they frequently get paid less for doing the same job.

Actually, pay equity is relevant to this entire issue. It's well known and commonly accepted that one's worth in the workplace is based on how much one gets in his or her paycheck. If women were paid equally for equal work, their status in general and their respect level among their male peers would rise, making them less susceptible to degrading insults and behavior.

Unfortunately, one of the avoidance mechanisms too many men use is to ignore the subject altogether. That's no answer either. Face it. Discuss it. Resolve it. One of the most discouraging events at the Thomas-Hill hearings was when Justice Thomas said that he tried and tried and tried to figure out why Ms. Hill could have possibly accused him of harassment. Then he added that he never even listened to her testimony. If he *really* wanted to know how and why it happened, he would have listened and tried to understand. Kind of makes one wonder if the real reason he didn't listen to her testimony was that he had already heard all the remarks the first time they were uttered—10 years ago when *he* said them.

The verbal battles can go on forever, and people can *talk* about possible solutions, but if any given workplace wants to really deal with the issue, there are some actions to take. As a start, every work group should take half a day to discuss this topic. The get-together should be jointly planned by the highest-level male and female in the organization.

Among women there should be a lot of, "Here is what you say, and here is why I don't like it." And men should be able to say,

"Well, here is why I say it and what I mean or don't mean by it."
And all concerned should decide on a set of behavioral guidelines
that can work. It's not easy, but more necessary than most people
think.

Margaret Mead might have had the real answer to the entire
issue: "The only real difference between men and women is the
way each contributes to the production of the next generation."

Some of the more insightful companies have been able to deal
with the entire issue of discrimination and harassment by getting
to the bigger issue: equal treatment at all levels of the organization. Lynn Bignell, a principal in the New York executive-
recruiting firm Gilbert Tween Associates, indicates that "companies have not made females a part of the mainstream."

In a recent *New York Times* article, Claudia H. Deutsch reviewed how some major companies are trying to change that and
at the same time how they are succeeding in reducing discrimination and sexual-harassment incidents. Management teams have
been established specifically to search out and correct the neglect
of females in workplace decisions.

Monsanto Co., for example, has trained employees to mediate
workplace disputes. Xerox and AT&T have encouraged women
to provide advice and critiques to management. The results have
been productive, since women no longer feel they are on the
outside looking in. Xerox actually has a bonus program for managers who are alert to females with potential for advancement.

Anne B. Fritz, a divisional manager for AT&T, sums up her
firm's approach: "We're looking at it, and we care." That attitude
may ultimately be *the* answer to the entire sexual-harassment and
discrimination issue—not just handling complaints, but changing
attitudes about the importance of women in the workplace.

III. WORK AND THE FAMILY

EDITOR'S INTRODUCTION

The percentage of traditional breadwinner-homemaker families in the United States has fallen from 70% in 1940 to about
20%. If there is no longer a full-time homemaker present, who is
doing the housework? Despite having entered the work force,
most women are still doing the housecare and child-care. This
makes them less competitive in the workplace. In the first selection, sociologist Arlie Hochschild argues in a chapter from her
landmark study, *The Second Shift,* that women from two-career
families are caught between "two competing urgency systems"—
at home and the office. There is no magic solution except the
hard work of negotiating a shift in long-established gender roles,
so that the real career cost of having a family can be more evenly
distributed.

As part of the shift away from breadwinner-homemaker families, more and more women are becoming single parents, over
one quarter of all births in 1990 were to unmarried mothers. The
second article in this section, "For Women, Varied Reasons for
Single Motherhood," describes why women become single mothers and suggests that sometimes there is no alternative. The rise
in single motherhood means that more and more women are in
the breadwinner role. Therefore, we must reconsider the definition of a family—it can't be assumed that a woman is providing
merely "a second income."

This presents a dependent-care problem on a very broad
scale. What can we do about it? "Who Helps Women Care for the
Young and the Old?" offers a feminist critique of governmental
and workplace response to the need for child-care and elder-care.
Written from the point of view of social workers, this article
points out that work-family needs of the middle class are very
different from those of the majority of Americans, and that national policy must take both into account. Should women be dependent on employer benefits, as detailed in the next selection,
"What Price Child Care?". The problem lies in the fact that busi-

ness may not be able to address the needs of the work-family on a broad enough scale.

Events in early 1993 have made it obvious that the provisions for child-care in the United States are not only haphazard but are also fraught with outdated regulations. President Clinton's initial nominee for Attorney General, Zoe Baird, withdrew her name from consideration after it was discovered that she had hired illegal aliens to care for her son, and then did not pay or properly report taxes on the money she paid them. The media's coverage of Ms. Baird's illegal activities made it clear to all that an employer is obligated to file an income tax return for anyone that he/she pays more than $50 a quarter.

THE WORKING WIFE AS URBANIZING PEASANT[1]

Women's move into the economy is the basic social revolution of our time. It embraces the lifetimes of Nancy Holt, Nina Tanagawa, Anita Judson, their mothers and grandmothers. Nancy Holt is a social worker and mother of two. Her mother was a Nebraska housewife and mother of four, and her grandmother raised five children on a wheat farm. Nina Tanagawa is an executive and mother of two. Her mother ran the house, raised three children, and helped keep the books in her father's hardware store. Her grandmother raised chickens and cows on a farm. Anita Judson is a billing clerk, mother of three. Her mother worked two jobs as a domestic and raised four children. Her grandmother worked a farm in Louisiana. Working from the present generation back, there is often this pattern of working mother now, urban housewife thirty years ago, farm woman fifty years ago. Sometimes two generations of urban housewives precede the farm woman, sometimes none. All these women worked. What's new is that, in taking paid work outside the home, masses of women live a life divided between two competing urgency systems, two clashing rhythms of living, that of the family and the

[1]From *The Second Shift* by Arlie Hochschild and Ann Machung, pp. 239–256. Copyright © 1989 by Arlie Hochschild. Reprinted with permission of Viking Penguin.

workplace. What's new, in scale at least, is childcare for pay, the massive spread of the double day, and the struggle within marriage to equalize the load at home. What's new is the pervasive *effect* of the struggle on the rest of family life.

This recent change is an extension of an earlier industrial revolution. Before the industrial revolution in America, most men and women lived out their lives on the private family farm— where crops were grown and craft work done mainly for domestic consumption. With industrialization, more crops and goods were produced and distributed to wider markets for money. But industrialization did not affect men and women at the same time or in the same way. It has affected men and women at different times and in different ways. In a sense, there is a "his" and a "hers" to the history of industrialization in America.

Painting the picture in broad strokes, the growth of factories, trades, and businesses in early American cities first began to draw substantial numbers of men and women away from farm life around the 1830s. Many single girls worked in the early New England textile mills for four and five years until they married, but mill girls represented a tiny fraction of all women and less than ten percent of all those who worked for wages. In 1860, most industrial workers were men. Only 15 percent of women worked for pay, most of them as domestic servants. As men entered factory work, they gradually changed their basic way of life; they moved from open spaces to closed-in rooms, from loose seasonal time to fixed industrial time, from life among a tight circle of kinsfolk and neighbors to a life of more varied groupings of kin and neighbors. At first, we might say, men did something like trying to "have it all." In the early New England rural factories, for example, men would work in these factories during the day and go home in the evenings to work in the fields. Or they moved in and out of factory work depending on the season and the crop ready for harvest. But over time, the farmer became an urban worker.

On the whole, the early effects of industrial employment probably altered the lives of men in a more dramatic and immediate way than it altered the lives of women, most of whom maintained a primary identity at home. To be sure, life changed for women, too. Earlier in the century, a young mother might churn butter and raise chickens and hogs. Later in the century, a young mother was more likely to live in the city, buy her butter and eggs at the grocery store, take in boarders, be active in the church, and

subscribe to what the historian Barbara Welter has called a "cult
of true womanhood" centered in the home, and based on the
special moral sensibility of women. Through this period, most
women who married and raised children based their role and
identity at home. "Home" changed. But, as the historian Nancy
Cott argues in *Bonds of Womanhood*, throughout the nineteenth
century, compared to men, women maintained an orientation
toward life that was closer to what had been. Thus, if we compare
the overall change in the lives of married women to the overall
change in the lives of married men, we might conclude that during this period men changed more.

Today, it is women whose lives are changing faster. The expansion of service jobs has opened opportunities for women. Giv-
en that women have fewer children now (in 1800 they gave birth
to about eight and raised five or six to adulthood; in 1988, they
average less than two) and given that their wage has been increasingly needed at home, it has become "the woman's turn" to move
into the industrial economy. It is now women who are wrenched
out of a former domestic way of life. If earlier it was men who
tried to combine an old way of life with a new one, now it is
women who are, by trying to combine the duties of the housewife
and full-time mother with an eight-hour day at the office.

In the early nineteenth century, it was men who began to
replace an older basis of power—land—with a new one—money.
It was men who began to identify their "manhood" with having money in a way they had never done before. Through the
great value on a man's purchasing power, the modern wor-
ship of goods—or what Karl Marx criticized as a "commodity
fetishism"—became associated with "being a man."

Today, it is women who are establishing a new basis of power and
identity. If women previously based their power mainly on attrac-
tiveness to men or influence over children and kin, now they base
their power more on wages or authority on the job. As Anita Judson,
the billing clerk married to the forklift driver, commented, "After I
started earning money, my husband showed me more respect."
Given the wage gap, and given the greater effect of divorce on
women, the modern woman may not have a great deal more power
than before, but what power she has is *based* differently.

Altering her source of power, earning money also gives some
women, like Carol Alston, a new basis of identity. As Carol, the
systems analyst whose husband did carpentry around the house
and helped a lot in a "male" way, described her reaction to quitting work after the birth of her first child, "I really discovered

how important it was to my identity to earn money." While earning money didn't make Carol feel more like a woman in the same sense that earning money made Ray Judson feel more like a man, earning money was more important to her identity than it had been to her mother's. Furthermore, the greater autonomy that often comes with working outside the home has probably changed the identity of women such as Carol to the same extent that it earlier changed that of men.

Housewives who go out to paid work are like the male farmers who, in an earlier era, left the country for the city, farm for factory. They've made an exodus "for the city." If earlier it was men who changed the social patterns of their fathers faster than women changed those of their mothers, today it is women who are changing these faster.

Paid work has come to seem exciting, life at home dull. Although the most acceptable motive for a woman to work is still "because I have to," most of the working mothers I talked to didn't work just for the money. In this way they have begun to participate in a value system once exclusively male and have developed motivations more like those of men. Many women volunteered to me that they would be "bored" or would "go bananas just staying home all day," that they were not, on any permanent basis, the "domestic type." This feeling held true even among women in low-level clerical jobs. A nationwide Harris poll taken in 1980 asked women: "If you had enough money to live as comfortably as you'd like, would you prefer to work full time, work part time, do volunteer-type work, or work at home caring for the family?" Among working women, 28 percent wanted to stay home. Of all the women in the study, including housewives, only 39 percent wanted to stay home—even if they had enough money to live as comfortably as they liked. When asked if each of the following is an important reason for working or not, 87 percent of working women responded "yes" to "providing you with a sense of accomplishment and personal satisfaction," 84 percent to "helping ends meet," and 81 percent to "improving your family's standard of living." Women want paying jobs, part-time jobs, interesting jobs—but they want jobs, I believe, for roughly the same complex set of reasons peasants in modernizing economies move to the cities. (In the United States we speak of farmers, not "peasants." The term *farmer* connotes free ownership of land, and a certain pride, while the term *peasant* suggests the humility of a feudal serf. I draw the analogy between modern American women and the modernizing peasantry because women's inferior social, legal, educational, and economic position had until recently been like that of peasants.)

In many ways, the twentieth-century influx of married women into an industrial economy differs from the earlier influx of men. For one thing, through the latter half of the nineteenth century up until the present, women's tasks at home have been reduced. Store-bought goods gradually replaced homespun cloth, homemade soap and candles, home-cured meats, and home-baked bread. More recently, women have been able to buy an array of preprepared meals, or buy "carry-out," or, if they can afford it, to eat out. Some send out clothes to a "wash and fold" laundry, and pay for mending and alterations. Other tasks women used to do at home have also gradually come to be done elsewhere for pay. Daycare for children, retirement homes for the elderly, homes for delinquent children, mental hospitals, and even psychotherapy are, in a way, commercial substitutes for jobs a mother once did at home.

To some extent, new services and goods have come to be preferred over the older domestic ones. Products and services of the "native" housewife have given way to mass production outside the home. Store-bought clothes, utensils, and foods have come to seem just as good if not better. In the two-job couple this trend moves even faster; working couples do less at home and buy more goods and services instead. A woman's skills at home are then perhaps also less valued. One working mother remarked: "Sometimes when I get upset and want to make a point, I refuse to cook. But it doesn't work. My husband just goes and picks up some Colonel Sanders fried chicken; the kids love it." Another mother said, "When I told my husband I wanted him to share the laundry, he just said, 'Let's take it to a laundry.'" The modern industrial versions of many goods and services come to be preferred over the old-fashioned domestic ones, even as colonial cultures came to prevail over old-fashioned "native ways." Just as the First World has raised its culture over the Third World's indigenous culture, so too the store-bought goods and services have marginalized the "local crafts" of the housewife.

The Housewife and the Working Woman

Not only are many of the products and services of the home available and cheap elsewhere, the status of the full-time housewife has been eroded. As the role of housewife has lost its allure, the wives who "just" stay home have developed the defensiveness of the downwardly mobile. Facing the prospect of becoming a housewife after quitting her job, Ann Myerson said, "If you want to know what shunning feels like, go to a cocktail party, and when they ask you what you do, say 'I'm a housewife.'" One illustration in the November 1970 issue of *True* magazine sums up the housewife's predicament: a commuter train is filled with businessmen reading morning newspapers and office memos. A bewildered middle-aged housewife in bathrobe and furry slippers, hair in curlers, searches the aisles for her husband, his forgotten briefcase in hand. Her husband is hiding behind his seat, embarrassed that his wife looks so ridiculous, so out of place. In their suits, holding their memo pads, reading their newspapers, the men of the commuter car determine what is ridiculous. They represent the ways of the city; the housewife represents those of the peasant.

Working mothers often feel poised between the cultures of the housewife and the working man. On one hand, many middle-class women feel severely criticized by relatives or neighbors who stay home, and who, feeling increasingly threatened and militant about their own declining position, inspect working mothers with critical eye. Nina Tanagawa felt the critical eye of the nonworking mothers of her daughter's friends. Jessica Stein felt it from affluent neighbors. Nancy Holt and Adrienne Sherman felt scrutinized by their mothers-in-law. Some of these watchful relatives and neighbors cross over the big divide themselves. When Ann Myerson's mother was a housewife, she criticized Ann for her overzealous careerism, but when her mother got a job herself, she questioned Ann's decision to quit.

At the same time, many working mothers seemed to feel both superior to housewives they know and envious of them. Having struggled hard to achieve her position as a systems analyst, Carol Alston didn't want to be confused with "ordinary" women who had not. Whenever she saw a housewife with a child, Carol recalled thinking, Why isn't she doing something *productive*? But seeing housewives slowly pushing their carts down the aisle at the Safeway at midday, she also questioned her own hectic life. When she dropped out of her "real" job to consult part time and care for her two children—and crossed the deepening rift—she began to sympathize with housewives.

Women who've remained back in the "village" as housewives have been burdened with extra tasks—collecting delivered par-

cels, letting in repairmen, or keeping afternoon company with
the children of neighborhood mothers who work. Their working
neighbors seldom have time to stop and chat or, sometimes, to
fully return favors.

Their traditional source of honor, like the peasant's, has been
threatened. In a preindustrial setting, a woman's claim to honor
was based primarily on her relation to her husband, her children,
her home. As the cash economy spread, money has become the
dominant symbol of honor and worth. Unpaid work, like that of
housewives, came to seem like not "real" work. The housewife
because "just a housewife," her work became "just housework." In
their book *For Her Own Good*, Barbara Ehrenreich and Deirdre
English have described how at the turn of the century, the Home
Economics Movement struggled against the social decline of
the housewife by trying to systematize and upgrade the role
into a profession. Women, its leaders claimed, could be dignified "professionals" in their own homes. Ironically, the leaders
of the Home Economics Movement thought housework was
honorable—not because it was *intrinsically* valuable—but because
it was just as real as *paid* work, a concession revealing how much
moral ground had been lost already.

Class Differences

If working wives are the modern-day urbanizing peasant,
then there are important differences between some "peasants"
and others. In addition to the split between housewives and working women, this social revolution also widens a second split
among women—between the women who do jobs that pay
enough to pay a baby-sitter and the women who baby-sit or tend
to other home needs. Carmen Delacorte, who sat for the children
of two other families I talked to; Consuela Sanchez, the Nicara-
guan woman who baby-sat for the Livingstons' daughter and
whose mother was raising Consuela's child back in Nicaragua; the
Myersons' Filipino baby-sitter, who had an eight-year-old daughter in the Philippines; the Steins' housekeeper and assistant
housekeeper: all these women are part of a growing number of
workers forming an ever-broadening lower tier of women doing
bits and pieces of the housewife's role for pay. Most likely, three
generations back, the grandmothers of all these women—
professional women, baby-sitters, housekeepers—were housewives, though perhaps from different social classes. Since class

has a remarkable sticking power, it may be that the granddaughters of working-class housewives moved into the economy mainly as maids, daycare workers, laundry and other service workers—doing low-paid "female" work—while the granddaughters of upper-middle and upper-class housewives tended to move in as lawyers, doctors, professors, and executives—doing mainly high-status "male" (and some "female") professional work. The granddaughters of the middle class may have tended to move into the expanding world of clerical jobs "in between." There is an important class difference between Carmen Delacorte and Ann Myerson: both form part of the new "peasantry," but as in the industrial revolution of the nineteenth century, some newcomers to the city found it much tougher going than others, and were more tempted to go home.

Preserving a Domestic Tradition?

But many women of every social class and in every kind of job are faced with a common problem: how shall I preserve the domestic culture of my mother and grandmother in the age of the nine-to-five or eight-to-six job? In some ways, the experience of Chicana women condenses the experience of all working women. Many Chicanas have experienced the strains of three movements—that from rural to urban life, from Mexican to American life, and from domestic work to paid employment. In her research on Chicana working women, the sociologist Beatrice Pesquera discovered that many conceived it to be their job as women to keep alive *la cultura,* to teach their children Spanish songs, stories, religious rituals; to teach their daughters to cook tortillas and chile verde. Their task is to maintain an ethnic culture eroded by television and ignored by schools in America. The Chicana considers herself a cultural bridge between present and past and this poses yet another task in her second shift. When they don't have time to be the bridge themselves, Chicana working mothers often seek a "tortilla grandma" to baby-sit and provide *la cultura.* Many white working mothers have fought a similar—and often losing—battle to carry forward a domestic culture—a culture of homemade apple pie, home-sewn Halloween costumes, hand-ironed shirts. On weekends and holidays most working women revert to being housewives.

Many traditional women such as Carmen Delacorte and Nina Tanagawa feel they should carry on *all* of the domestic tradition.

To them, the female role isn't simply a female role; it is part of a cultural tradition, like a rural or ethnic tradition. To the traditional, it seems that *only women* can carry on this tradition. Having secured a base in the industrial economy, having forged a male identity through their position in that economy, men have then relied on women to connect them back to a life outside it. In *The Remembered Gate*, Barbara Berg argues that as Americans moved off the land, the values of farm life moved into the home. The woman at home became the urban agrarian, the one who preserved the values of a bygone rural way of life while living in the city. By "staying back" in this sense, she eased the difficult transition for the men who moved ahead. Who is easing the transition for women now?

Although traditional women want to preserve the "domestic heritage" their mothers passed on, most working mothers I talked to felt ambivalent about it. "Do I really *need* to cook an elaborate meal every night?" they ask themselves. Cutting back on tasks at home often means working mothers are not living up to their mothers' standards of care for home or child, nor to the collective female tradition of the recent past. One woman summed up the feelings of many others: "I'm not the type that has to see my face in the kitchen floor. That part of my mother's cleaning routine I can let go, no problem. But I don't give my child as much as my mother gave me. That's why I want my husband involved—to make up for that."

Some men have responded to the declining domestic culture, much as colonizers once responded to the marginalization of traditional peasant life. Secure in their own modern culture, the colonizers could collect peasant rugs, jewelry, or songs, or cultivate a taste for the indigenous cuisine. Today, some successful professional men, secure in their own modern careers, embrace a few tokens of the traditional female culture. They bake bread or pies on Saturdays, or fix a gourmet meal once a month. But very few men go completely "native"; that would take at least an extra month a year.

Unequal Wages and Fragile Marriages

Women's move into the economy, as a new urban peasantry, is the basic social revolution of our time. On the whole, it has increased the power of women. But at the same time, other realities lower women's power. If women's work outside the home increases their need for male help inside it, two facts—that women earn less and that marriages have become less stable—inhibit many women from pressing men to help more.

Today, women's average earnings are only a bit higher, relative to men's, than they were a hundred years ago; for the last hundred years women have earned 60 percent of what men earn; today it's 70 percent. Given this difference, women still have more of an economic need for marriage than men do.

Meanwhile, what has changed is the extent to which a woman can depend on marriage. The divorce rate has risen steadily through the century and between 1970 and 1980, it actually doubled. Experts estimate that 49 percent of all men and women who marry today are likely to divorce sometime before they die. Whatever causes divorce, as the sociologist Terry Arendell points out in *Divorce: Women and Children Last,* the effect of it is much harder on women. Divorce usually pushes women down the class ladder—sometimes way down. According to Lenore Weitzman's *The Divorce Revolution,* in the first year after divorce women experience a 73 percent loss in standard of living, whereas men experience a 42 percent gain. Most divorced men provide surprisingly little financial support for their children. According to the Bureau of the Census in 1985, 81 percent of divorced fathers and 66 percent of separated fathers have court orders to pay child support. Twenty percent of these fathers fully comply with the court order; 15 percent pay irregularly. (And how much child support a father pays is not related to his capacity to pay.)

Most divorced fathers have distressingly little emotional contact with their children as well. According to the National Children's Survey conducted in 1976 and 1981 and analyzed by sociologist Frank Furstenberg, 23 percent of all divorced fathers had no contact with their children during the past five years. Another 20 percent had no contact with their children in the past one year. Only 26 percent had seen their children for a total of three weeks in the last year. Two-thirds of fathers divorced for over ten years had not had any contact with their children in more than a year. In line with this finding, in her study of divorced women, sociologist Terry Arendell found that over half of the children of divorced women had not received a visit or a call from their father in the last year; 35 percent of these children had not seen their fathers in the last five years. Whatever job they took, these women would also have to be the most important person in their children's lives.

Arendell also found that many middle-class divorced women didn't feel they could turn to their parents or other family members for help. Thus, divorced women are often left in charge of the children, are relatively poorer—often just plain poor—and often lack social and emotional support. The frightening truth is that once pushed down the class ladder, many divorced women and their children get stuck there. This is because they have difficulty finding jobs with adequate pay and because most of them have primary responsibility for the children. Also, fewer divorced women than men remarry, especially older women with children.

While women's entrance into the economy has increased women's power, the growing instability of marriage creates an anonymous, individualistic "modern" form of oppression. In the nineteenth century, before a woman could own property in her own name, get a higher education, enter a profession, or vote, she might have been trapped in a marriage to an overbearing husband and have had nowhere else to go. Now we call that woman "oppressed." Yet today, when a woman can legally own property, vote, get an education, work at a job, and leave an oppressive marriage, she walks out into an apparently "autonomous" and "free" form of inequality.

Divorce is an undoing of an economic arrangement between men and women. Reduced to its economic bare bones, traditional marriage has been what the economist, Heidi Hartmann, calls a "mechanism of redistribution": in a sense, men have "paid" women to rear their children and tend their home. In the late nineteenth and early twentieth centuries, unions fought for and won a higher "family wage" for male workers, on the grounds that men needed the money more than women in order to support wives and children. At that time it seemed reasonable that men should get first crack at the better-paying jobs, and even earn more than women for doing the same work because "women didn't support a family." Since this arrangement put men and women in vastly unequal financial positions, the way most women got a living wage was to marry. In the job market, the relation between men and women was as the upper to the lower class in society. Marriage was the economic equalizer.

But as marriage—this "mechanism of redistribution"—has grown more fragile, most divorced men still earn a "family wage" but no longer "redistribute" it to their children or the ex-wife who cares for them. The media stresses how men and women both have the freedom to choose divorce, and surely this choice is an important advance. But at the same time, the more men and women live outside marriage, the more they divide into separate classes. Three factors—the belief that childcare is female work, the failure of ex-husbands to support their children, and higher male wages at work—have taken the economic rug from under that half of married women who divorce.

Formerly, many men dominated women within marriage. Now, despite a much wider acceptance of women as workers, men dominate women anonymously outside of marriage. Patriarchy has not disappeared; it has changed form. In the old form, women were forced to obey an overbearing husband in the privacy of an unjust marriage. In the new form, the working single mother is economically abandoned by her former husband and ignored by a patriarchal society at large. In the old form, women were limited to the home but economically maintained there. In the new form, the divorced woman does the work of the home but isn't paid for it.

The "modern" oppression of women outside of marriage has also reduced the power of women *inside* marriage as well. Married women are becoming more cautious, more like Nina Tanagawa or Nancy Holt who look at their divorcing friends and say to themselves, "Put up with the extra month a year or divorce? I'll put up with it."

The influx of women into paid work and her increased power raise a woman's aspirations and hopes for equal treatment at home. Her lower wage and status at work and the threat of divorce reduce what she presses for and actually expects.

The "new" oppression outside marriage thus creates a tacit threat to women inside marriage. Married women say to themselves, "I don't want what happened to her to happen to me." Among the working parents I talked with in this study, both men and women expressed sympathy for the emotional pain of divorcing friends. But women told these stories with more anxious interest, and more empathy for the plight of the divorced woman. For example, one evening at the dinner table, a mother of two who worked at word processing had this exchange with her husband, a store manager, and her former boss, as they were telling me about the divorce of a friend:

A good friend of mine worked as a secretary for six years, putting her husband through dental school. She worked like a dog, did all the housework, and they had a child too. She didn't really worry about getting ahead at the job because she figured they would rely on his work and she would stop working as soon as he set up practice. Well, he went and fell in love with another woman and divorced his wife. Now she's still working as a secretary and raising their little boy. Now he's got two other children by the other woman.

Her husband commented: "That's true, but she was hard to get along with, and she had a drinking problem. She complained a lot. I'm not saying it wasn't hard for her, but there's another side to the story."

The wife answered, surprised, "Yeah, but she was had! Don't you think?"

Her husband said, "Oh, I don't know. They both have a case."

Earlier in our century, the most important cautionary tale for women was of a woman who "fell" from chastity before marriage and came to a bad end because no man would have her. Among working mothers of small children, and especially the more traditional of them, the modern version of the "fallen woman" is the divorcée. Of course, not all women fear the prospect of divorce—for example, not Anita Judson. But the cases of Nancy Holt and Nina Tanagawa are also telling because their fear of divorce led them to stop asking for more help in the second shift. When life is made to seem so cold "out there," a woman may try to get warm inside an unequal marriage.

All in all, then, two forces are at work: new economic opportunities and needs, which draw women to paid work and which put pressure on men to share the second shift. These forces lend appeal to an egalitarian gender ideology and to strategies of renegotiating the division of labor at home. But other forces—the wage gap between men and women, and the effect on women of the rising rate of divorce—work in the opposite direction. These forces lend appeal to a traditional gender ideology and to the female strategy of the supermom and to the male strategy of resistance to sharing. All the couples I studied were exposed to both these sets of forces, though they differed in their degree of exposure: some women were more economically dependent than others; some were in more precarious marriages. It is the background of this "modern" oppression that made many women, like Carol Alston or Ann Myerson, feel very grateful for the men they had, even when they didn't share the whole strain of the second shift.

The Haves and Have-Nots of Backstage Support for Work

The trends I have described constitute the stall in the revolution and stack the cards in favor of husbands not sharing the second shift with their working wives. Once all these forces are set in motion, one final pattern keeps men doing less: women's lack of "backstage support" for their paid jobs.

It sets up a cycle that works like this: because men put more of their "male" identity in work, their work time is worth more than female work time—to the man and to the family. The greater worth of male work time makes his leisure more valuable, because it is his leisure that enables him to refuel his energy, strengthen his ambition, and move ahead at work. By doing less at home, he can work longer hours, prove his loyalty to his company, and get promoted faster. His aspirations expand. So does his pay. So does his exemption from the second shift.

The female side of the cycle runs parallel. The woman's identity is less in her job. Since her work comes second, she carries more of the second shift, thus providing backstage support for her husband's work. Because she supports her husband's efforts at work more than he supports hers, her personal ambitions contract and her earnings, already lower, rise more slowly. The extra month a year that she works contributes not only to her husband's success but to the expanding wage gap between them, and keeps the cycle spinning.

More than wages, what affects a man's contribution at home is the value a couple puts on the husband's or wife's job. That judgment depends on the investment in education, the occupational status, and the future expectations each partner has with regard to the other. In general, the more important a man's job, the more backstage support he receives, and the less backstage support for her job a woman receives, the less important her job becomes.

The inequality in backstage support has received little notice because most of it is hidden from view. One cannot tell from sheer workplace appearance who goes home to be served dinner and who goes home to cook, any more than we can tell rich from poor these days just by how people dress. Both male and female workers come to work looking the same. Yet one is "poorer" in backstage support than the other. One irons a spouse's uniform, fixes a lunch, washes clothes, types a résumé, edits an office memo, takes phone calls, or entertains clients. The other has a uniform ironed, a lunch fixed, clothes washed, a résumé typed, an office memo edited, phone calls taken, and clients entertained.

Women (with traditional or transitional ideologies) believe they ought to give more backstage support than they get. Career-centered egalitarian women gunning for promotion feel they deserve to receive as much as they give. But family-oriented egalitarians—men and women alike—aren't eager to clear the decks at home for more time at the office. They consider the home as their front stage. The rise of the two-job family has reduced the supply of housewives, thus increased the demand for backstage support, and finally somewhat redistributed the supply of that support.

There is a curious hierarchy of backstage "wealth." The richest is the high-level executive with an unemployed wife who entertains his clients and runs his household; and a secretary who handles his appointments, makes his travel arrangements, and orders anniversary flowers for his wife. The poorest in backstage support is the single mother who works full time and rears her children with no help from anyone. Between these two extremes lie the two-job couples. Among them, the husbands of working wives enjoy less support than husbands of housewives, and the men whose working wives do all the second shift enjoy more support than men who share. In general, men enjoy more support than women, and the rich enjoy more of it than the poor.

In a study I did of the family life of workers in a large corporation, I discovered that the higher up the corporate ladder, the more home support a worker had. Top executives were likely to be married to housewives. Middle managers were likely to be married to a working spouse who does some or most of the housework and childcare. And the clerical worker, if she is a woman, is likely to be single or a single mother and does the work at home herself. At each of these three levels in this company, men and women fared differently. Among the female top executives, 95 percent were married to men who also worked and 5 percent were single or single parents. Among male top executives, 64 percent were married to housewives, 23 percent were married to working wives, and 5 percent were single or single parents. So compared to men, female top executives worked in a disadvantageous environment of backstage support. As one female manager remarked: "It's all men at my level in the company and most of them are married to housewives. But even the ones whose wives work seem to have more time at the office than I do." As women executives at this company often quipped, "What I really need is a wife."

In the middle ranks, a quarter of the men were married to housewives, nearly half were married to working wives, and about a third were single. Among women in the middle ranks, half were part of two-job couples and carried most of the second shift. The other half were single or single parents. Among lower-level clerical workers, most were single or single mothers.

Being "rich" or "poor" in backstage support probably influences what traits people develop. Men who have risen to the top with great support come to be seen and to actually be "hard driving," ambitious, and "committed" to their careers. Women who have had little support are vulnerable to the charge of being "uncommitted." Sometimes, they do become less committed: Nancy Holt and Nina Tanagawa withdrew their attention to work in order to take care of "everything else." These women did not lack ambition; unlike Ann Myerson, their work felt very real to them. They did not suffer from what the psychologist Matina Horner calls a "fear of success," in her book *Women's Will to Fail*. Rather, their "backstage poverty" raised the emotional price of success impossibly high.

In an earlier economic era, when men entered industrial life, their wives preserved for them—through the home—a link to a life they had known before. By "staying back" such wives eased a difficult transition for the men who were moving into the industrial age. In a sense Nancy Holt is like a peasant new to a factory job in the city; she is part of a larger social trend, doing what others like her are doing. In the nineteenth century, men had women to ease the transition for them but in the twentieth century, no one is easing the transition for women like Nancy Holt.

FOR WOMEN, VARIED REASONS FOR SINGLE MOTHERHOOD[2]

Houston—Vice–President Dan Quayle issued a blunt reminder last week that after 25 years of cultural warfare over the American family, single mothers were likely to remain a divisive topic because their lives illuminate unresolved differences between the races and the sexes.

In a speech on Tuesday, Mr. Quayle argued that the riots in

[2]Article by Roberto Suro. From *The New York Times* p.A12 My 26 '92. Copyright © 1992 by The New York Times Company. Reprinted with permission.

Los Angeles were "directly related to the breakdown of family structure, personal responsibility and social order in too many areas of our society."

But his remarks will be best remembered for the connection he drew between poor, unmarried black mothers and Murphy Brown, an affluent, white television character who he said mocked "the importance of fathers by bearing a child alone and calling it just another 'life style choice.'"

Census Bureau statistics and studies by social scientists suggest that there are few generalizations to be made about single mothers except that their numbers have been increasing for 20 years, although at a slower rate recently.

Varied Needs, Varied Choices

Interviews conducted around the country with single mothers of varying races and economic conditions suggested that the decision to bear a child involves a mixture of practical, emotional and spiritual considerations and is usually not a straightforward moral choice.

For Jean Pollard it was not a matter of choice at all. "He wasn't a planned child," Ms. Pollard, 34 years old, said of her 3-month-old son who lives with her in a shelter for homeless families in Houston. She was laid off from work, she said, and then the child's father reneged on a promise to marry her.

"I wanted kids, but I always figured when I had a child I would be married, the typical American dream," she said. "Sometimes it doesn't work out like that."

Like many single mothers, Ms. Pollard acknowledges the value of marriage. But she went on, "Marriage doesn't guarantee anything anymore because it's not like it used to be with our parents."

For Debbie Spain, staying married was not an option.

A 32-year-old medical secretary in Boston, Ms. Spain was beaten by the father of her first child and ended a brief marriage to her second child's father, who was an alcoholic. "Just because you have someone's last name doesn't mean that's going to solve any problems," she said.

Both of her children remain in close contact with their fathers, but Ms. Spain finds they are happier now that she is raising them alone. "I just decided I'm going to do it right as much as I can," she said.

For Patty Friedmann, having a child was more important than having a husband.

Ms. Friedmann, a 45-year-old writer in New Orleans, deliberately became pregnant when she was single and 28 because she wanted a child. In an autobiographical novel published last year by Viking, "The Exact Image of Mother," Ms. Friedmann, who is now married, described how women can assert their identities by making such choices.

Of her protagonist, Ms. Friedmann wrote, "She is unfocused in life and in conflict with her mother, and her decision to have a child brings her strength and her resources together and defines her."

The many different reasons that women give for being single mothers suggest that their lives reflect a variety of trends in American life.

"You can't isolate single parenting by women as a discrete phenomenon," said Barrie Thorne, a professor of sociology at the University of Southern California. "You have to see it in the context of an overall change in attitude towards many sexual and family issues including the status of women, divorce and premarital sex."

Census Bureau statistics show a period of turmoil in the American family beginning in the mid-1960's, although the rate of change in family composition slowed markedly in the 1980's. Married couples with children, for instance, made up 40 percent of all households in 1970 but only 26 percent last year.

Single parenthood by unwed mothers rose quickly, and is still increasing. The number of families headed by mothers who have never married increased at annual rate of nearly 15 percent in the 1970's. Although the rate dropped to just under 10 percent from 1980 to 1991, this now constitutes the fastest growing category of family groupings.

Single mothers now head a quarter of all families with children, counting those have never married along with women who are divorced, widowed or are living apart from a spouse for any other reason. (There are single fathers, too, of course, but they head fewer than 4 percent of all families.)

Experts say that although economic circumstances have changed since the 50's, the "Father Knows Best" family—two parents with only the husband working—that typified that decade still exerts a powerful pull on American values and emotions. Large majorities in opinion polls consistently say they are committed to conservative views of the family like those articulated by Mr. Quayle, and the vast majority of children continue to live in households with two parents.

But, said Arlene Skolnick, a research psychologist at the University of California at Berkeley, "People often care deeply in opposing directions, such as believing in the 1950's family but also accepting the value or the necessity of women working outside the home."

Aside from this complex cultural context, Professor Thorne said, "there are structural and circumstantial problems that go beyond individual choices that help explain why families headed by single parent mothers are not only the most rapidly growing type of household but also the type most associated with poverty."

Felicia Bryant, 19, of Chicago spoke of the devastating impact an unwanted pregnancy can have on a poor woman.

On learning she was pregnant, Ms. Bryant said: "I was upset and shocked. I wanted to commit suicide. I felt that I was too young to have a child." Then 15 years old, she dropped out of school and went on welfare.

Although Mr. Quayle asserted that "marriage is probably the best anti-poverty program of all," Ms. Bryant did not see it as an antidote.

"Many of the homeless are whole families—men, women and children—and they are still in poverty," she said. "A man can lose a job anytime. A man is not always the best means of support. A woman can be just as independent as a man."

An Old Phenomenon

The birth of children outside marriage, especially among the poor, is neither particularly new nor peculiarly American. Historians and social scientists note that industrialization and urban growth often coincide with changes in family structure.

These situations have often produced criticism similar to Mr. Quayle's. Social critics in 19th century Britain, for example, spoke of "the undeserving poor" and argued that out-of-wedlock births were a result of immorality.

In America the issue is complicated by race. While single parenting by mothers has increased quickly among both whites and blacks, it is far more prevalent among blacks. In 1991, women headed 58 percent of all black families with children, as against 19 percent among whites.

And there are major differences between blacks and whites in the reasons women head families.

Among white mothers, the major reasons are divorce and separation, although the number who have never married has increased rapidly, from less than 3 percent of one-parent families in 1970 to 19 percent last year.

Among black mothers, divorce and separation also used to be the major causes for single parenthood, but no more. Last year 54 percent of one-parent black families were headed by women who had never married. This was up from just 15 percent in 1970, according to the Census Bureau.

"Poverty, unemployment, welfare programs that penalize families: these things explain a major portion of the variance between blacks and whites in the number of female headed households, but not all of it," said Bonnie Thornton Dill, a professor of women's studies at the University of Maryland in College Park.

One explanation may lie with changes in the nature of urban poverty that have led to an increasing number of people cut off from the education or employment that might allow them to improve their status or give them the impetus to marry.

"Teen-age pregnancy among blacks has not increased so much, but the rate of marriage among teen-agers has dropped and the number of children born to married couples has dropped," Professor Dill said. "These things are related to perceptions of opportunity."

Perceptions of another sort also emerged as a major theme in interviews with single mothers, who argued that although their households may not be considered conventional they are nonetheless real families.

Grace Cox, a 35-year-old typographer in Houston, has one child from an early marriage that ended in divorce and another born to her as a single mother.

"When you have kids by yourself, you have to work harder at making sure they have what they need and at keeping the family together," she said.

Like several other women, Fran Ramer, a 42-year-old Chicago businesswoman who is a single mother, said she was deeply committed to the family as a social ideal and saw herself adapting that ideal to reality.

She said, "I don't disagree with Quayle about family values,
but I think he is a little behind the times about what a family is."

WHO HELPS WORKING WOMEN CARE FOR
THE YOUNG AND THE OLD?[3]

Dependent care, meaning responsibility for the care of members of society who because of age or other circumstance are
unable to care for themselves, has become a highly visible
socioeconomic-political issue in the past 10 years. Most of the
attention has been devoted to deploring the situation of young
children who do not have a 24-hour, at-home parent, but the
plight of older adults who are no longer able to maintain themselves independently is increasingly being addressed. This article
analyzes governmental and workplace responses to these issues
and proposes that women should become leaders in finding solutions that are woman friendly, as well as family friendly.

Nationally, in 1991, 75 percent of women aged 20–44 were in
the labor force, including more than half the women with children younger than age 6 (and those younger than age 1). Over 28
million children of working mothers required child care by 1988.
Furthermore, of the 42 million Americans who were 60 years or
older in 1991, 90 percent lived in the community, either alone or
in families, but it is not known how many required help with the
tasks of daily living, ranging from minimal oversight to 24-hour
care. Estimates of the number of caregivers of the elderly who are
employed women vary from 20 percent to 40 percent of the female work force; 75 percent of the persons who provide care to
elderly family members (hereafter called "eldercare") are women
(Administration on Aging [AOA], 1991; "More Choose to Stay
Home with Children," 1991; Williams, 1991).

These are the bare statistical outlines of the old and young
populations who need dependent care and of those who provide
that care. However, the recital of numbers hardly suggests the

[3]Article by Betty Sancier and Patricia Mapp. From *Affilia* 7/2:61–76 Summer
'92. Copyright © 1992 by Women & Social Work, Inc. Reprinted with permission of
Sage Publications, Inc.

vast personal, political, and policy ramifications for American families of fulfilling some of the most basic functions of families in any society: to nurture and socialize the young, to succor the ailing, and to provide care for those who are too old and frail to maintain their independence.

Wisconsin, which enjoys a reputation as a state with progressive policies, is typical in its demographic characteristics. Therefore, in this article, governmental policies and responses of employers to family-workplace issues in Wisconsin are analyzed to illustrate some of the advances and impediments to alleviating the stress of holding a job while caring for family members that working women experience.

Background

The Industrial Revolution detached the worker and paid work from the home, ushering in the massive social revolution that permanently affected all aspects of living. The meanings of time, work, family relationships, standards of living, roles and responsibilities, education, the tenor of daily life, class relationships, and basic values were all reordered and changed forever (Abramovitz, 1988).

Among the consequences that followed the severing of the workplace-family tie were the following:

• "Work" became a paid activity, carried out away from the worker's residence. Conversely, the activities that took place in the home became less visible and were no longer considered "work" in the sense of productive activity (Sapiro, 1990).

• Men, by and large, were the "workers" who left their homes each day. The collective activities of the women who spent their days working in those homes, called "housework," commanded neither wages nor status—a situation that still exists (Sapiro, 1990).

• Until recently, the bargain between workers and employers was financial. It was virtually unthinkable for family issues to be the subject of more than the most casual exchange between employers and employees. Employee assistance plans (EAPs), inaugurated about 20 years ago to help alcoholic employees, signaled the beginning of the work-family connection. EAPs and human resources departments in many organizations have now expanded their scope to encompass a comprehensive array of work-family concerns (Kamerman & Kahn, 1987).

• Although women have entered the labor force in large numbers, they continue to perform household tasks and to care for the young and old. The multiple roles and burdens that women carry have been well documented. To date, however, women have not had the power and influence in government or at work to shape practical solutions that are based on their perceptions of their needs and wants (Boneparth, 1982; England & Farkas, 1986).

Who Cares?

Women care. Gilligan (1982) identified an ethic of care as the key element of women's moral development. Often misinterpreted, this concept has been used to glorify self-sacrifice by women. As Hooyman (1990, p. 231) pointed out, "Caregiving is an expected duty for women . . . [but] an unexpected expression of compassion by men." This patriarchal society officially recognizes the social need to *care about* children and the elderly by assigning women to *care for* them. The women who began careers in the past 15 years have been taught that private and voluntary solutions to their caregiving needs are preferable to governmental intervention in family life. Piecemeal, fragmented, expensive, difficult-to-locate programs are what they find and what they have come to expect (Aldous, 1990; Kamerman & Kahn, 1987). Western European nations, in contrast to the United States, routinely provide children's allowances, family leave, day care, and other benefits that are designed to make family life more manageable for workers (Hewlett, 1986).

Women do not, by and large, wish to abandon their caring roles; however, they urgently need to find ways to become instrumental in determining the circumstances and conditions under which they can both care for those who are dependent on them and work outside the home. Otherwise their lives will continue to be characterized by stress and confusion, as they seek personal rather than structural solutions to persistent work-family problems (Kaden & McDaniel, 1990). At present, the government and employers, not women themselves, are providing the main impetus for defining dependent-care options pertaining to both children and the elderly.

Feminist Issues in Dependent Care

The term *work-family issues* is still widely understood to be shorthand for issues that are of primary concern to women: child care, parental leave, and eldercare. Public policy and employers consider these issues to be problems that *female* workers bring to the workplace (Daniel, 1987; Epstein, 1970; Kamerman & Kahn, 1987).

In at least four crucial areas, American feminists have not endorsed clear proposals to interpret and meet the daily needs of women in the work force. Opportunities have been lost that might have benefited many women. First, feminists have been reluctant to endorse the Western European pattern of supports for working mothers. Feminist dogma has held that gender-neutral legislation is the best route to equality. The fear is not unfounded that protective measures directed toward women may backfire in further discrimination. Nevertheless, feminists must pursue a better balance between long- and short-range measures if they wish to be instrumental in the work-family arena in the coming decade (Stetson, 1991).

Second, the mass media's attention continues to fasten on negative research findings about working mothers, and feminists have been unable to counter these results. Efforts to reframe the issues to eliminate the bias toward traditional families and to emphasize the strengths of diverse families are greatly underfunded and still in their infancy. Thus the single-minded insistence on "women's rights" in the workplace may now be a counterproductive strategy. Certainly, it is one that has alienated women who stay at home and who believe that their real stresses and problems have been trivialized. As a consequence, women who give up the fast track for domesticity are applauded and held up as models (Labich, 1991), which confirms that feminists have yet to make much of a dent in the cult of domesticity (Daniel, 1987).

Third, feminists must reconcile the fact that the work-family needs of middle-class, professional women and the majority of working women are different. Most of the family-friendly workplace policies that exist are designed for the former group. For instance, unpaid family leave requires sufficient reserves to support the family during the leave. Families who are living on the margin of solvency do not enjoy this luxury. Nor are the popular information-and-referral services of much use to parents who cannot pay for high-quality day care. Poor women, minority women, immigrants, and various other "deviants" are buffeted by highly derogatory and discriminatory policies and attitudes (Aldous, 1990).

Fourth, despite these persistent dilemmas, there is no platform to empower women to assert more control over the conditions of their work-home-family lives. Therefore, the responses of employers are uneven. Partial solutions maintain the economic status quo. Structural questions about the way work is organized fail to be raised, and the role of the government in providing minimal family benefits for all workers fades from view. One authority on family policy pointed out that feminists of various theoretical persuasions embrace divergent, sometimes contradictory, positions as they "analyze the relationship between the family, the economic and political structures of society, and the status of women" (Spakes, 1989, p. 10). Women are seldom heard when decisions are made.

Dependent-Care Benefits

In the past 10 years, generally speaking, the government and employers have endorsed only voluntary and private dependent-care programs. Conservative administrations have consistently opposed a governmental role in mandated parental leave, comprehensive high-quality child care programs, supports for families providing eldercare, and other proposals. Such initiatives are alleged to interfere with the family's prerogatives, on one hand, and with the workings of the free market, on the other hand. Welfare families, in contrast, experience massive governmental interference in their lives from experimental programs that are designed to prepare them for or push them into the labor market.

The government and employers endorse a smorgasbord of voluntary employer-sponsored programs to alleviate family-related stress on the job so that workers will be more productive to their employers. In a capitalist society, all benefits for workers must enhance profits. Employers are encouraged to provide information, referral, consultation, flextime, assistance for childcare or eldercare, reimbursement formulas, and other benefits, but not in any context of a national consensus on the realities of family life in the United States today, and not at the expense of profits (Biegel & Blum, 1990; Kamerman & Kahn, 1987; Scharlach, Lowe, & Schneider, 1991). Many experts doubt that the economy is capable of providing enough jobs at sufficiently high pay to bring poor women out of poverty.

These voluntary trends, which receive strong support from the mass media, give the impression that employers are enthusiastically participating in an array of comprehensive programs that are designed to improve the lot of (women) workers. The true picture is much more modest. In 1990, the U.S. Small Business Administration identified only 24 companies with under 200 workers that provided child care, and only 5,600 employers reported that they provided any financial support for child care. Typically, the firms that have responded to the needs of families in this area have experienced tight labor markets, have high profit margins, and enjoy a progressive managerial team (Friedman & Galinsky, in press).

Wisconsin has a proud history as a state with progressive social policies. This tradition has been partially eroded by antiwelfare sentiment and renewed support for the traditional patriarchal family. In the next section, recent experiences are cited to illustrate the strengths, weaknesses, and dilemmas of the most popular work-family programs and to illuminate the differential treatment accorded to women on welfare. Child care advocates in the state have been working with employers for over 10 years, and eldercare has been discussed in the past 3 years.

Wisconsin Confronts Dependent Care

Poor women who require public assistance fare poorly in their attempts to become employable while caring for their children. Wisconsin's welfare experiments, permitted through federal waivers of regulations for Aid to Families with Dependent Children (AFDC), have been the subject of considerable national notoriety. Workfare requires an AFDC parent with a child over age 2 to participate in training, job-seeking, and placement activities or risk losing benefits. Learnfare reduces the amount of the AFDC grant if a high school child is absent from school more than twice a month. "Bridefare," a new proposal for which the governor has requested a waiver, would provide an $800 per year bonus in benefits to eligible young parents who marry, provided no additional children are born (Task Force of the Women's Agenda, 1991).

Independent evaluations of workfare and learnfare are raising serious questions about the programs' efficacy, as opposed to their political appeal. Other states that are rushing to emulate Wisconsin would do well to heed the reservations, only two of which will be mentioned: (1) up to 25 percent of the families sanctioned by learnfare were known to be at risk of child abuse and (2) subjects in the control group were just as likely to become employed as were those who were receiving training through workfare (Murphy, 1991; Quinn, Pawasarat, & Roehrig, 1991; Pawasarat & Quinn, 1990; Sandin, 1991; Stanford, 1991; Taylor, 1991).

The commitment to move welfare mothers from public assistance to paid employment is more than clear; it is strident. Yet buried in self-righteous calls for "strengthening traditional families" and "restoring the work ethic" are bleaker realities. Wisconsin enjoyed a stable economy during the 1980s and has had an unemployment rate (4.6 percent) that has been lower than the national average for more than two years ("Employment Trends," 1991–92; Task Force of the Women's Agenda, 1991). Nevertheless, in Milwaukee County, the number of poor working families rose by 63 percent between 1980 and 1990, and 53 percent of the female-headed households were living in poverty in 1990. Furthermore, in 1990, licensed child care spaces were available to only about 20 percent of the Milwaukee children who required care, including the AFDC children whose parents were required to be in the job market (Task Force of the Women's Agenda, 1991).

Moreover, there is no reason to suppose that low-income women or those on AFDC are less involved in caring for elderly dependent relatives than are other employed women. In fact, some authorities suggest that eldercare is even more stressful than is child care (Friedman & Galinsky, in press; Naples, 1991).

Clearly, advocates in Wisconsin have not been notably successful in stemming the tide of antiwomen, antipoor, implicitly racist programs that have mistakenly been heralded as "pro-family." They have, however, been able to capitalize on the wish of the government and employers to appear family friendly toward traditional working families. State appropriations for child care services have expanded, and some employers have introduced other child care benefits. A few employers are beginning to look at the need for eldercare (Sancier & Mapp, 1991).

The Wisconsin Manufacturers and Commerce (WMC) commissioned surveys of its members in 1985 and 1989 to gather information about dependent-related benefits being offered to employees (Mapp, 1990). The response rates were 30 percent (276) in 1985 and 22 percent (418) in 1989. The changes reported over time were taken as an indication of the degree of commitment and the potential for change.

The four key elements that Friedman (1983) defined as crucial for balancing work and family are used to analyze the survey

TABLE 1.   Time-Off Benefits Reported by WMC
Respondents: 1985 and 1989 (in percentages)

Year	Maternity Leave	Part-Time Work	Flextime
1985	57	61	35
1989	81	65	48

SOURCE: Mapp (1990).

responses and to evaluate the relative merits of various benefits to employees. These elements are time off, information, services, and financial capacity:

• **Time Off** The principal time-off benefits for dependent care reported by WMC respondents in 1985 and 1989 are summarized in Table 1. During the same period, the proportion of employers that offered parental leave that included fathers doubled—from 16 percent to 39 percent—an advance attributable to the passage of the Wisconsin Family and Medical Leave Act of 1988, which requires certain employers to provide limited leave for either parent following the birth or adoption of a child (Mapp, 1990).

Kingston (1990, p. 447) questioned whether the benefits of flexible arrangements are real or illusory: "The extra time that part-time work makes available for domestic life generally involves an unappealing trade-off, costing workers so much in basic financial terms that any gains to the quality of family life are severely undercut." However, when queried at the Conference Board's 1991 seminar on balancing work and family ("Mainstreaming," 1991), three teams of managers and their female subordinates who were representing successful "flexible partnerships" reinforced the personal advantages while shrugging off the reality that the women were working far more hours than called for by their part-time compensation.

• **Information** Although different options for time off for dependent care are most widely available, the possibility of addressing family needs through the distribution of information on balancing work and family has the most potential, according to employers in Wisconsin. In both 1985 and 1989, over 70 percent of the employers in the WMC surveys said they "would consider or are considering" providing such information, while less than

10 percent actually did so (Mapp, 1990). However, neither information dissemination services nor resource-and-referral services
are universally available for employers to use even if they opt for
them as low-cost, low-risk concessions to the dependent-care
needs of workers.

Only 7 percent of the employers in the 1989 WMC survey
offered a referral service, typically through a national provider
that was linked with a local child care coordinating agency to
counsel parents. Although resource-and-referral, or consultation, services are a model by which information on eldercare and
child care may be disseminated to employees, the provision of
such services may obscure and delay the consideration of funda-
mental issues, such as the need for higher wages that would enable employees to pay for high-quality services.

• **Services and Financial Capacity** Child care is the third-
highest expense for families who use it, exceeded only by housing
and food (Friedman, 1983). It is not surprising that financial
assistance and actual child care services, which are the most expensive services, are least developed by employers. Moreover, high-
quality services, defined here as regulated care (certified by a
county or licensed by the state and provided by trained staff), are
the exception in Wisconsin and elsewhere. In any case, only .4
percent of the WMC respondents provided financial assistance for
child care in 1985, and 2 percent provided it in 1989, a statistically
impressive 500 percent increase, but in reality, minimal progress.
Similarly, the proportion of employers who provided on-site child
care rose from .4 percent to 2 percent during the same period. The
number of programs more than doubled—from 35 to 90, but few
employees and their children benefited, considering that there
were 115,720 employers in Wisconsin in the fourth quarter of 1990
(Wisconsin Department of Industry, Labor and Human Relations,
December 1991, personal communication).

Data on employer's responses to eldercare needs in Wisconsin
hardly even qualify as minimal. The topic was not mentioned in
the 1985 WMC survey. In 1989, 70 percent of employers expressed interest in learning about the experiences of other companies but only 39 percent said they "might be interested" in how
to design and conduct a survey of employees' needs in this area.

National Picture

These statistics should not be misconstrued as a systematic trend
toward accommodating women with children in the workplace.

Eldercare is barely understood as a concept. Most of the gains in Wisconsin and elsewhere have been in the health care industry, where labor shortages have forced hospitals and nursing homes to adopt competitive practices to attract workers who are mothers.

National reports bear out the meager progress documented by the Wisconsin survey. For example, the U.S. Department of Labor reported in 1988 that of the 1.2 million companies that employed over 10 persons, only 2 percent offered employer-sponsored child care and more than 50 percent of employed mothers were not covered by maternity leave policies (Galinsky & Stein, 1990). Thus the family-friendly benefits for women who are in the mainstream labor market are often more illusory than substantive. Moreover, women who are attempting to become self-sufficient while they care for their families often cannot find adequate family supports or other than poverty-level jobs.

Why has there been such negligible response by employers when the proportion of employed women with young children doubled from 30 percent in 1950 to 60 percent in 1989? Part of the answer is that both employers and employees have faith in the workings of the free market. Employers who believe that the laws of supply and demand should govern wages and working conditions resist offering expensive frills that will cut into profits (Galinsky & Stein, 1990). Employees who have endured systematic "givebacks" of long-established benefits are understandably loath to make new demands.

Since the era when organized labor won concessions (life insurance, health insurance, and paid sick leave and vacations) for male breadwinners, there has been no noteworthy parallel progress in the provision of dependent-care services that would permit women to be equal partners in the world of work. Unions, employers, and policymakers alike continue to discount the importance of women workers speaking and acting to influence change in their own behalf.

The slight gains just cited and the attendant focus by the mass media on a few employers who provide exceptional benefits should not deflect feminists from striving to change the status quo. Rather, the gaps noted in this article provide an opportunity to advance the cause of working women.

Feminist Visions of Benefits

In the best of all possible feminist worlds, there would be a harmonious melding of productive work and individual, family, and community activities. More immediately, the following issues in practice, in public policy, and in the workplace require prompt action by feminists.

• Social workers in occupational settings should sensitize themselves to the realities of the lives of women workers and begin to involve women in exploring creative organizational solutions to their dependent-care needs. Support groups, lunchtime seminars, and informal meetings provide opportunities to add organizational problem solving to the more traditional personal agendas.

• Counselors and therapists should pay more attention to the work-related aspects of their clients' lives, encouraging clients to consider how to modify their work environments, as well as their personal behavior.

• Social workers who work with unions or who are union members should insist that organized labor make dependent care a priority.

• Researchers must reframe their investigative agendas. What are families who are successful in juggling work and family life doing right? Profiles of all types of working families are needed, with no bias toward the traditional family form.

• Feminist organizations, such as the National Organization for Women must focus on economic issues for all women. The most salutary possible benefit for low-income women would be stable jobs paying good wages. The women would then be able to afford child care, eldercare, respite care, and many other services to relieve their stress.

• Gerontologists, caregivers, and others must push for a sound, thorough, factual woman-oriented data base on employed caregivers of the elderly to provide the necessary documentation for action by employers and the government.

• Feminists must advocate for the special needs of different groups of women. They should focus on enabling unemployed single parents to obtain jobs without sacrificing their children.

• Long-range solutions must include the advancement of a feminist agenda on employment. Professional associations and women's organizations must promote women's political participation and leadership and, most critical, must work to get women elected to public office.

Conclusion

Women have not yet achieved the power to control and define their own life course, nor will the formidable impediments embedded in a patriarchal society soon dissolve. Therefore, they must strive to overcome the serious block to progress that is represented by their inability to come together on work-family issues and must become the agents who define and determine work-family conditions, rather than continue to be objects of the idiosyncratic free market. It is time to make visible the hidden hand of the "free-woman economy," in which women initiate the changes they define for themselves and their families.

The key to universalizing the appeal of a feminist worldview remains elusive. Perhaps the vision is too grandiose. However, the issue of dependent care, now in the national consciousness, is fluid enough to provide an opportunity for feminists to reframe its significance in ways that will make dependent care the *feminist* issue of the 1990s.

WHAT PRICE CHILD CARE?[4]

When S. C. Johnson & Son decided in 1985 that it needed to offer employee child care to attract and retain top talent to its bucolic Racine (Wis.) headquarters, it didn't scrimp. Today, 400 children from newborn to age 12 use Johnson Wax's state-of-the-art child-care center in a company-owned park with boating lake and Olympic-size swimming pool. Not only is care offered before and after school for older kids, there's even day camp during school vacations. The cost for day care—$90 to $115 a week—is less for employees making under $60,000 annually. "This isn't a benefit—it's a good business decision because we want to attract the best," says JoAnne Brandes, an attorney and a founder of the program. "I only wish they had this when my child was born."

If only every parent today had that kind of safety net. But for most working parents, child care these days doesn't work. Costs vary wildly among regions. Quality is spotty and often not policed. And, unlike most Western nations, the U.S. provides only minimal child-care assistance to all but the poorest families.

Actually, this should come as no surprise. America simply never planned for the dramatic march of women into the work

---

[4]Article by James E. Ellis with Judy Temes and Joan O'C. Hamilton. From *Business Week* F 8 '93. Copyright © 1993 by McGraw-Hill, Inc. Reprinted with permission.

force during the 1980s. Fully 55% of women with young kids
work today, double the level of 1973. Yet the nation still clings
to the old every-woman-for-herself method of securing child
care that depended heavily on nearby relatives to baby-sit
junior.

Zoë Baird's failed nomination as U.S. Attorney General thrust
the child-care debate into the spotlight. She knowingly employed
an illegal alien to care for her child—a situation thousands of
other families share as well. But that choice is forcing most working parents, employers, and even governments to grapple with a
vexing challenge: rethinking how America cares for its young—
and who will pay for that care.

That won't be easy, but society has little choice. Employees are
being forced to look beyond salaries and place a value on family
benefits such as flexible hours. Employers, especially those that
depend on a female work force, must cope with the costly absen-
teeism and high turnover spawned by inadequate child care. And
government is confronted with an increasingly vocal middle class
that sees a big chunk of the good life leave every month in child-
care payments.

There's certainly no shortage of proposals. They range from a
sharply increased child-care tax credit to even requiring child
care by employers. But there is a shortage of the one thing that
makes such care more accessible: money. The federal government, which spends upwards of $1.5 billion annually on child-
care programs, is deep in debt. The states, which share in the cost
and administer many low-income programs, are also strapped.
Even healthy businesses are loath to offer what can become an
ever more-costly benefit.

Ironically, availability isn't the major problem nationwide. In
many regions, there's actually a surplus of child-care slots—a reason big chains such as Kinder Care Learning Centers Inc. and La
Petite Academy Inc. have been weak performers in recent years.
"Child-care centers all over the nation are 70% full, so there's
plenty of capacity," says Jack L. Brozman, president of Kansas
City-based La Petite Academy, the nation's second-largest child-
care chain. "The real issue is affordability."

Still, shortages do exist in metropolitan areas such as New
York and San Francisco, where high land costs make centers too
expensive to build. Also, local health-and-safety ordinances often
make child care even more costly. Mothers of infants—whose care
is more expensive—complain loudest of difficulty finding help.

Last summer, Cheryl Wilhelmi left her job as director of a Denver art school to live as a full-time mom in a former stagecoach stop near Roundup, Mont., partly because she couldn't find the right person to care for her twin infant daughters in her home. She had read many stories about child abuse and was wary of day-care centers that weren't employer-sponsored. "I could not see myself loading those two babies into infant seats every day and leaving them at day care," says Wilhelmi.

Although there was financial sacrifice in her career change, Wilhelmi's artist husband does hold a job. But most working women, especially single parents, don't have a choice to stay at home when child-care options aren't to their liking. Half of the women who return to welfare do so because of child-care problems. And affordability is not just the poor's problem: Robin Means, director of the Union Theological Seminary Day Care Center in Manhattan, says her center averages a $1,000-a-month fee for full-time infant care, which often eats up 75% of the take-home pay of the second spouse in two-income families. That leads to desperate measures. "Some use their student loans to pay for child care," says Means.

The care Americans expect is often more than they can afford. Working women in the U.S. routinely pay 25% of their take-home pay for child care. And even the grandmom next door—if she's willing to risk cutting her Social Security payouts by reporting babysitting income—can charge $125 a week.

More women are turning to their employers for solutions. Last fall [1992], a consortium of 137 companies and nonprofits formed the American Business Collaboration for Quality Dependent Care (BW, Sept. 28). Its goal: to raise $25 million to fund child- and elder-care projects. And Johnson Wax isn't the only stellar success. Corning Inc. started funding a day-care center in 1979 and today handles 120 kids in two day-care programs as well as 160 kids in after-school programs daily.

But companies don't have to go that far to make a difference. Morrison & Foerster, a San Francisco law firm with offices nation-wide, found that on-site centers just wouldn't work. Some parents just didn't want to commute with kids. But they were generally worried about having emergency care. So the firm subsidizes child-care costs during child illness or sudden business trips.

Even the most ardent advocates of increased child care know that business can't carry the load alone. Millions of parents work at companies that are either too small or too poor to provide services. That's left many parents anxiously looking toward a cash-strapped Washington for help.

Still, there are things the feds can do at relatively modest expense. Childcare advocates say more federal funds could be targeted for junior college programs that train infant-care workers, perhaps enrolling welfare mothers in those programs. That would not only alleviate the most pressing need but also help other women leave the public dole. Cities, too, could step in. Baltimore lets private operators pay nominal rents for public school buildings to run daycare centers. The program has brought more than 1,000 new child-care providers into its licensing system.

But such piecemeal measures—generally aimed at the poor— aren't good enough in the eyes of the middle class. "It would be unheard of anywhere in Europe to expect families to be solely responsible for the burden of child care," says Karen Nussbaum, executive director of 9 to 5, National Association of Working Women.

Besides granting 360 days of paid parental leave after the birth of a child, Sweden offers subsidized daycare at municipally run centers. Federal and local governments split 90% of the costs, with parents paying 10%. As a result, 85% of Swedish women work outside the home.

France goes even further, providing free, universal care for children above the age of three, and it heavily subsidizes care for younger kids. But such comprehensive welfare programs mean that France spends roughly $200 billion on child care and on extensive welfare programs for families, double what the U.S. pays for similar benefits, figures American University economist Barbara R. Bergmann. France does have twice the toddlers per teacher vs. a typical American center. But "France is a less affluent country, and they do it," says Bergmann. "It's not a question of having adequate resources, it's a matter of allocation of resources."

That seems to be the nut of the problem. The nation is far from a consensus on whether providing care should be a governmental responsibility. "If an employer and its unions negotiate child-care benefits, that's fine," says Murray Weidenbaum, former chairman of President Ronald Reagan's Council of Economic Advisers. "But why get the government involved and have working women without children subsidize those that have them?"

That's really a political question—and a potential middle-class bombshell. But don't look for Washington to answer it anytime soon. Congress revamped federal daycare funding just two years ago. And with President Clinton focused on the deficit, child-care reform isn't even on the back burner. Unless lawmakers pass a more cohesive program, it's up to business to fill the vacuum. Until companies—and the government—devise better choices, the real casualties from the child-care mess won't be superstars such as Zoë Baird, but everyday working families and their children.

BABY SITTERS' BOSS TELLS ALL[5]

Dear I.R.S.:

In all this flap over Zoë Baird and her illegal Peruvian couple, a few facts about what we parents owe the I.R.S. got clarified. It turns out—gosh, I really had no idea—that I should have been filing a tax return for anyone who works in my house who earns more than $50 a quarter. That doesn't include what you call Independent Contractors—recognizable because they bring their own tools. So I can skip the plumber, the exterminator and the guys from the Christian Brothers Cleaning Company, who shampoo the wall-to-wall carpet. (Christian, as in Born Again. They take prayer breaks.) But there are a lot of others. Not because I'm in the big time, domestically speaking. I'm no Zoë Baird with two full-time helpers. Rather, like lots of Americans, I use a patchwork of sitters. I just can't quite get this child-care thing streamlined.

I realize I've been shirking my responsibilities, and I'd like to set about rectifying that immediately by confessing and filing.

So here goes. Up to the start of 1992 I always had an au pair to take care of my two children, now ages 6 and 9, while my husband and I were at work. The au pairs were legal, part of an I.R.S.-and-Immigration-approved program. Unfortunately, we moved last year and lost our extra bedroom. Our fifth and final au pair returned to Ireland at the end of 1991.

[5]Article from *The New York Times Magazine* p.14 F 7 '93. Copyright © 1993 by The New York Times Company. Reprinted with permission.

In January I hired a woman from Brooklyn, an American citizen, to pick up my children at school at 3 and baby-sit till 6:30. At $7.50 an hour, she earned $131.25 a week. She had children of her own and was eligible for Medicaid, which she would have lost if she declared the income from the job with me. On March 10, after she failed to show up for the third time, I fired her. Actually, I had also begun to suspect, from the number of phone calls from men that inundated our house every afternoon, that she was running another business on the side. Andy, the carpenter who was trying to make a closet into a bedroom for our son—he brought lots of tools, believe me—was of the same opinion. Maybe she could have afforded health insurance after all.

I was pretty frantic after dismissing her, and so when a friend suggested that a young woman she knew named Alecksandra could fill in for a couple of months, I said yes. Alecksandra, I have to admit, was an illegal alien—from Cróatia. She'd come as a legal au pair a few years earlier when her country was still Yugoslavia, and now although she wanted to go home, she agreed to stay here, at her parents' urging, until summer, when they hoped things might be calmer. She'd most recently been working for a family from 8 to 6, including housecleaning, for $60 a week. Alecksandra was nice—and available—and really needed a job, so I hired her. On Memorial Day weekend, she and her boyfriend went to Niagara Falls. She decided it would be fun to cross the bridge into Canada. Needless to say, Immigration would not permit her to return. You can reach her in Zagreb, or possibly in Berlin, where I think she has since emigrated.

In some desperation, I turned to Barnard College, which has a baby-sitting service. There I found Gail, who was looking for a short-term job. I paid her a total of $495 for three weeks' part-time work.

Before I forget, I should mention the neighbor who comes once a week to clean. She is an American citizen married to the Sardinian super in the building up the street. She works around her children's school schedules, which means not during the summer, Christmas or spring vacations. At $60 a week, her total comes to $2,160 for the year.

On June 15, the kids began attending the summer day program run by a nearby church, tax ID number 13-2870343. I was completely legal for two and a half months.

Every once in a while, we go out at night, and then we hire a young French friend, at $7.50 an hour. For a five-hour evening out, that comes to $37.50. Our friend, also an illegal alien, is applying for a student visa. She comes for Christmas and birthdays, as a guest—no pay, I promise. I'll have to go over my calendar to add up her total hours of baby-sitting.

In July a friend lent us his house on Cape Cod, and when we left we hired the wife of the motel owner down the road to clean. We paid her $60. I can't remember her name but the motel was called something like the Sea Pines, in Truro. Or maybe it was the Whispering Pines. Well, she had red hair. I wish I could say she brought her own rag mop, but she didn't.

For September and the beginning of the new school year, I decided to really get organized. I hired two baby sitters from Barnard, one from Boston, to work Monday, Tuesday and Friday afternoons, and one from New York, to work Wednesday and Thursday. For three afternoons, Boston gets paid $90. For two, New York gets $55. So that's a total of $1,530 for Boston, $990 for New York.

Boston was out sick for a week in December and her roommate Bob filled in, so that's $90 for Bob. I don't know his last name but he lives in the East Village.

Let me see. That's the woman from Brooklyn, Alecksandra, Gail, the neighbor who cleans, the friend from France, the Motel-Keeper's Wife, the Barnard girl from Boston, the Barnard girl from New York and Bob.

I called Jim Weikart of Weikart Tax Associates, who tells me I need the following forms. To start with, an SS-4, to apply for an Employer Identification Number. I also need—one for each employee—I.R.S. Form 942 to be filed quarterly with payments totaling 15.3 percent of wages in Social Security and Medicare taxes. Four copies per employee of the W-2 form. The W-3 Form, which is the cover for the W-2. I only need one W-3 for all the W-2's. And I need a Federal Unemployment Form 940-EZ.

Now—whoops, I guess it's a little late for this—but Jim says I was also required by law to have the woman from Brooklyn, Alecksandra, Gail, the neighbor who cleans, the friend from France, the Motel-Keeper's Wife, the Barnard girl from Boston, the Barnard girl from New York and Bob fill out W-4 forms before they began work, as well as a Form I-9, stating that they're American citizens. And of course they should have been filing their 1040's. Let me know what I owe.

This doesn't concern you, but Jim says we also have to file New York State Unemployment IA 5 quarterly, and WT-4-A and

4-B annually, to report how much, if any, I'm withholding in New York State and City taxes (does that mean I don't *have* to do this?). I may also have to file New York State Workers' Compensation and Disability Insurance forms, depending on the number of hours an employee works. Jim isn't sure, since this isn't taxes.

I know I'm late getting to this, but I really want to come clean. As of March 30, 1993, you'll be getting my quarterly forms. Assuming all remains stable in my house, I'll be filing for the neighbor who cleans, the friend from France, the Barnard girl from Boston, the Barnard girl from New York, Bob and the Motel-Keeper's Wife, since we plan to go back to Cape Cod for a week in July. That's at least five Federal forms per worker, one filed quarterly and one sent to four different places, and three state forms for each filed quarterly, adding up to 138 forms total for the year. For me.

The neighbor who cleans, the friend from France, the Barnard girl from Boston, the Barnard girl from New York, Bob and the Motel-Keeper's Wife will also be filing. By my calculation, you and the state will be getting 42 forms from them.

Gee, it strikes me that I may have to hire somebody full time before I get to this. And you all at the I.R.S. will probably need to do some hiring to handle the paper work too. Just think what we both will be contributing to combating unemployment.

IV. THE NEW POLITICS

EDITOR'S INTRODUCTION

There are several factors that account for the sudden visibility of women in the 1992 political campaign. Even before the Thomas-Hill hearings of the previous year there was a growing discontent with the status quo among the electorate—the economy had deteriorated, various scandals had rocked the Congress, and disagreements between the Republican administration and the Democratic Congress had led to legislative gridlock. The end of the Cold War caused a shift in national priorities to domestic issues. The election, under any circumstances, would have been a good opportunity for outsiders. The Senate Judiciary Committee appeared on a national television and implied that Professor Anita Hill was lying or crazy, as she recounted her alleged sexual harassment by Clarence Thomas while they both worked at the Equal Opportunity Employment Commission. Contributions to EMILY's List (a Democratic women's political action committee) rose by 50% in the two months following the hearings. A generation of woman politicians, who were ready for their next challenge, walked through the open door.

The first selection, "Crashing the Open Door," by Wendy Kaminer, outlines some of the obstacles that women face in their political careers. What are the specific fundraising and credibility problems that women encounter? Should women be elected because they are women? The second selection, "The Year of the Sexist Women," outlines how these gender-specific campaigns, because they confirm stereotypes, rather than encourage voters to view a candidate as an individual, may do more harm than good.

Women's political actions committees, such as EMILY's List and WISH were very successful at raising funds in 1992. "The Year of the Woman" by William McGuren, points out that they are not purely gender-specific groups but also have a pro-choice agenda in their selection of candidates. Mr. McGuren contends that the "Year of the Woman" is not about gender but ideology.

The final article in this anthology, "Did America 'Get It'?" by
Eloise Salholz, examines the triumphs and disappointments of
1992. What is Anita Hill's legacy? Ms. Salholz asserts that it may
be some time before we have a complete answer to that question.

CRASHING THE LOCKER ROOM[1]

In her thirteen years as a senator from Arkansas, Hattie Caraway, the first woman elected to the U.S. Senate, made only fifteen
speeches on the floor. "And they say women talk all the time," she
wrote in her diary, after listening to her colleagues' orations. A
former housewife who inherited her husband's seat in 1931 and
was re-elected to it twice, Caraway was known as Silent Hattie or
The Woman Who Holds Her Tongue. "I haven't the heart to take
a minute away from the men," she explained. "The poor dears
love it so."

Telling me this story at the outset of an interview, Nancy
Kassebaum, a Republican senator from Kansas, at first seemed
like Hattie Caraway, less embittered than bemused by the male
monopoly on the Senate. Although she and the Maryland Democrat Barbara Mikulski are the only two women in the Senate today
[1992], she does not, she told me, wish for more women senators
so much as she wishes for more moderate Republican ones. She
called herself a U.S. senator, not a woman senator, in comment-
ing on her vote in favor of Justice Clarence Thomas's nomination
to the Supreme Court, and she said she has not felt disadvantaged
by her sex in any of her campaigns or committee assignments.
Kassebaum sits on the Senate Foreign Relations Committee, over-
seeing a traditional male preserve. Still, she mused, men's voices
do have more authority on foreign-policy issues. "There's an indifference to the contributions one can make," she said, only a
little obliquely. "What I can resent is indifference"—which apparently extends even to areas in which women might be expected to
have considerable expertise.

"I was never once asked by anyone at the White House or by
any of my colleagues about how I reacted to Anita Hill's public

---

[1]Article by Wendy Kaminer. From *The Atlantic* 270/1:58–67 Jl '92. Reprinted
with permission.

allegations of sexual harassment or how I thought the allegations should be handled, which was kind of interesting," Kassebaum recalled.

Both Kassebaum and Mikulski, however, were invited to sit with the Judiciary Committee during the Thomas-Hill hearings. Both declined. "Barbara and I felt it would have been demeaning," Kassebaum explained. Mikulski, who voted against the Thomas confirmation, was a little more direct when I spoke with her: "I was not on the committee. It was not my job to give an imprimatur to the hearings. It was not my job to prop them up or do a whitewash."

Precisely what other role the two women senators might have played on the committee was unclear. Their invitation was issued in haste, on the morning of Hill's testimony, when Mikulski called Senator Joseph Biden to protest the proceedings. (She previously had asked for a delay to investigate the allegations.) "It was fifteen minutes before the hearings began!" she exclaimed. "I wasn't even in Washington; I was in Baltimore." Sometimes, as Nancy Kassebaum says, there's indifference.

That the Senate is indifferent to women's voices and concerns is the kindest interpretation of the Thomas-Hill hearings offered by many women. Male senators tended to ignore or trivialize the charges of sexual harassment—because, Bella Abzug, the former New York congresswoman, asserts, "they do it all the time." Abzug echoes a common refrain. "It's a way of life for them." Ellie Smeal, the founder of The Fund for the Feminist Majority, is blunter, recalling what a male lobbyist once told her about male legislators: "They fish together, they hunt together, they play cards together, and they whore together."

Whether or not outrage over the Thomas-Hill hearings is confined to politically active professional women, as some claim, whether or not that outrage will affect the upcoming election (it has already cost Alan Dixon, an Illinois Democrat who voted for Thomas, his seat, and may defeat Arlen Specter, of Pennsylvania, as well), whether or not the public had its collective consciousness raised by Hill's story and the commentaries it engendered, the televised hearings provided an emotionally charged image of the Senate as an exclusive club for white males of a certain age. The committee looked like an aging former football team from some segregated suburban school.

Of course, the exclusion of women from Congress is not exactly news; it's history. Only fourteen women have ever served in

the U.S. Senate, and the majority of them inherited their husbands' seats or were appointed for limited terms by governors
with whom they had political or personal connections. (Two governors have appointed their wives to vacant Senate seats: Edwin
Edwards, of Louisiana, in 1972; and Bibb Graves, of Alabama, in
1937.) Only 117 women have served in the House since its incep-
tion. Out of 11,230 people who have served in Congress, only one
percent have been women. Today there are two women in the
Senate and twenty-eight women in the House (out of 435 members). In other words, women constitute 5.6 percent of Congress,
an increase of only about three percentage points since 1971.
Women have made considerably more progress at the state and
local level, suggesting that they face a glass ceiling in politics, as
they do in corporate life. [The 103rd Congress (1993–95) is
10.1% women with 48 women in the House and 6 in the Senate.]

But statistics are a bore; the Thomas-Hill hearings were en-
thralling, to partisans on either side. "I was as enraptured by the
hearings as anyone," Secretary of Labor Lynn Martin recalls.
"They were sirenlike." In a post-literate age the video images of
the Judiciary Committee were also powerfully persuasive; they
dramatized the homogeneity of the Senate more than statistics
and polemics ever could.

Someday Clarence Thomas's most fervent opponents may
thank him for his help in electing women to the Senate. As an
organizing tool, the Thomas-Hill hearings may do for women
politicians in the 1990s what *Roe* v. *Wade* did for the New Right in
the seventies. The dramatic upset primary victories of the senatorial candidates Carol Moseley Braun, in Illinois, and Lynn
Yeakel, in Pennsylvania; the record number of women running
for the Senate and the House; and record amounts of money
pouring into women's campaigns have been among the biggest
political stories of the year. Both Braun and Yeakel attribute their
candidacies to the Senate hearings. Not only did the hearings
make a lot of women angry but they "demystified the Senate,"
Braun says. "Instead of dignified men debating lofty issues, the
public saw garden-variety politicians making bad speeches."

The Problems Women Face

Why are garden-variety politicians invariably male? Why
aren't more women in the Senate? You might also ask, Why aren't
more women in corporate boardrooms, or at partnership meetings of major law firms?

You can usually predict the response to the question about women in the Senate (or the boardroom) if you know our respondent's ideology. Liberal Democrats and feminists talk about the ways in which women have been kept out of power by bias. Conservative Republicans and other traditionalists are likely to say that women have opted out, following a natural inclination to stay home. Moderates tend to focus on "structural" obstacles to women's political advancement—the power of incumbency and the fact that having entered political life in significant numbers relatively recently, women are still making their way up the hierarchy; women lack "bench strength," they say inside the Beltway. (The same explanation is often given for women's secondary status in the corporate world.)

The structural explanation sounds appealingly objective and is no doubt partly true, but it takes you back to your starting point. Why weren't women more active politically thirty years ago? Were they kept out of power or did they opt out, naturally? Do we have any basis for asserting what comes naturally to women when their choices have long been so unnaturally constrained?

The reasons for women's absence from the Senate are, of course, at least as complicated as the reasons for their absence from the upper echelons of most high-status professions. Socialization, custom, the division of labor within the home, access to contraception, some degree of choice, and, I suspect, considerable bias all play their roles. "The last time anything was simple, you were eight years old," Lynn Martin reminded me.

But to simplify just a little: Among political women and the experts who study them there is a clear consensus about the problems women candidates have traditionally faced. Again, people perceive bias through the scrim of ideology. More-conservative women candidates are likely to present it as a relatively minor problem; more-liberal candidates are likely to present it as a major one.

Talking to women from both parties, however, you hear complaints and observations about bias that are familiar to most professional women:

Women have a harder time than men establishing their credibility as candidates, because our traditional images of political leadership are male (along with our traditional images of trial lawyers and neurosurgeons). According to the Democratic pollster Celinda Lake, whose studies on women candidates are widely cited by Democrats, the credibility problem has "three prongs"—competence, electability, and toughness.

Men are presumed to be competent; women must prove they're competent. (Women internalize this message, some suggest, and think they have to be qualified to run; men just run.)

Women must also prove that they're viable candidates, capable of waging winning campaigns. This problem of proving electability is circular: women need to prove their viability to raise money, but they can't show that they're viable until they've raised money.

Women have a hard time proving that they're tough enough. Voters want candidates who will fight for them, but women who present themselves as fighters are likely to be considered strident, at best, or bitchy. Celinda Lake has observed, with apparently unintended poignancy, that a woman can also effectively establish toughness by pointing to some personal tragedy she's managed to overcome.

In addition to these general credibility problems (which seem to be lessening), women candidates also cite particular, familiar manifestations of bias. They commonly complain that the press pays too much attention to a woman's appearance. Josie Heath, a 1990 and 1992 Democratic senatorial candidate from Colorado, notes that she can describe her wardrobe by reading her campaign clips. Women are also plagued by questions about their marital status, no matter what it is. That a husband can be a serious liability was clearly shown by Geraldine Ferraro's vice-presidential campaign; Dianne Feinstein, the former mayor of San Francisco, and Josie Heath were also questioned about their husbands' finances. But the absence of a husband can be a liability too. Women candidates are "penalized by marriage," Barbara Mikulski says. "If you're married, you're neglecting the guy; if you're divorced, you couldn't keep him; if you're a widow, you killed him; if you're single, you couldn't get a man."

These problems of bias and the facts of family life underlie the primary structural obstacles to women's political advancement. Women tend to start their political careers later than men, after their children are grown, and so have less time to position themselves politically. Their place in the hierarchy and the presumption that women are not competent or electable make it difficult for them to raise money, and until recently fund-raising was cited as one of women's primary political problems. Fund-raising difficulties also reflect sex segregation throughout the job market (which is related, of course, to divisions of labor at home). Clustered in lower-paying jobs, women have less money to give to their candidates and causes. "Women tend to give in smaller amounts, and they give ideologically. They give for abortion rights or because they want to see someone fighting for Anita Hill," the Democratic consultant Nikki Heidepriem remarks. "Men tend to give for economic reasons, with an eye on the bottom line. The big money comes from entrepreneurs and corporate types who do business in Washington, and they tend not to be women."

The Parties as Locker Rooms

So what? Some men, and women, readers are probably impatient by now with these laments. Male candidates are not all well connected; they, too, have trouble raising money, challenging incumbents, and receiving what they consider fair treatment from the press. Appearance and image matter for men as well—graduate students in men's studies could write treatises on the politics of baldness. Minority men can probably point to at least as much bias as white women can (and have even less representation in the Senate). The generalizations about the special problems of women candidates are only generalizations. Each candidate has his or her own combination of advantages and disadvantages, involving not just sex and race or ethnicity but also geography, ideology, telegenicity, shrewdness, wit, personal history, and luck. Women complaining of bias don't deny this. They do claim that although the factors in each race are different, the balance of factors, particularly in statewide and federal elections, generally favors men.

The party apparatuses and operatives also favor men, particularly in the eyes of Democratic women. Republican women candidates don't as a rule offer much public criticism of their party, except perhaps on the issue of abortion. Democratic women don't as a rule offer much praise; instead, many scoff at the suggestion that their party is doing enough for women.

Levels of mistrust are high. Jane Danowitz, of the Women's Campaign Fund, is convinced that Dianne Feinstein would not have had a primary challenge in her bid this year for the California senate had she been a man. "Feinstein almost won the 1990 California gubernatorial race. She was the party's standard-bearer. Had she been a man, they would have cleared the field." Who's they? "You can start with George Mitchell [the Senate majority leader] and Chuck Robb [the head of the Democratic Senatorial Campaign Committee]. There is an old-boys' network that could have dried up the money for any other candidate entering the race." Kam Kuwata, Feinstein's campaign manager, dismisses this suggestion (as do a few other political women). The political director of the DSCC, Don Foley, stresses that the national party stays out of primary battles (as it is required to do). "They stay out officially but they go in the back door when they want," Danowitz charges.

The old boys, however, are beginning to change their ways, Danowitz adds. Since January of this year the DSCC has been holding unprecedented meetings with the women's political community and showing increasing concern for women candidates. Given the remarkable momentum of women this year, a resurgence of feminism, and a pervasive disgust for incumbents, it's fair to call this a foxhole conversion. Given the history of party politics, redemption may not be so easy.

Whether or not they believe that the party in effect conspires against them, women often describe it as a locker room. At the national level "both parties take a very conventional approach to recruitment," according to Anita Dunn, an aide to New Jersey Senator Bill Bradley and a former senior staffer at the DSCC. "They look at the governors and the visible congressmen. Recruitment is a very subjective process, depending on the same small, predominantly male circles. And if you're a Democrat, the conventional wisdom is that you shouldn't run a candidate who's perceived as liberal, as are most Democratic women in the House." Sometimes, Dunn adds, "'liberal' is a code word for 'woman.'"

At the state level the locker room is smaller and perhaps even more firmly established. New Jersey Republican Christine Todd Whitman, who ran a surprisingly close race against Bradley in 1990, believes that if the party had thought it had any chance of defeating Bradley, it never would have nominated a woman to run against him.

"All politics is local, and at the local level there's a group that says, 'We'll run Bob. He's my buddy,'" Colorado Congresswoman Pat Schroeder says. Schroeder recalls the party's "anointment" of Tim Wirth for the Senate seat that Gary Hart vacated in 1986. She had been in Congress longer than Wirth but, she says, was not even considered for the seat. "The party regulars said, 'We'll run Tim, he's our candidate, because it's so hard on him, having to raise money to run for the House every two years'—as if it's easy for me."

The implication of bias in Schroeder's story may or may not be fair, but it indicates a pervasive view of the parties as men's clubs in which women are only tokens. That view has led at least a few Democratic women to demand affirmative-action plans for candidates. "The parties say, 'We don't discriminate; women can run,'" Bella Abzug observes. "But we're running against the tide of history. It's not enough to say 'We don't discriminate.'" Women advanced professionally partly because of affirmative action, the argument goes; they may not advance politically without it.

In fact the Democratic Party does have an affirmative-action plan for delegates; devising a plan for candidates is a bit more problematic (as well as extremely unpopular). Affirmative-action plans for candidates may be feasible only in parliamentary systems, in which the parties run slates of candidates. But Abzug has a suggestion—or, rather, a demand. She has recently helped launch a campaign calling on the parties to nominate only women for open seats. "This may not be the idea that will do it, but I'm trying to get people to think creatively. I want people to be more creative and demanding."

Meanwhile, according to one Democratic consultant, "The Democratic Party has all it can do to get out of bed in the morning. You can say it's not doing much for women, but it's not doing much of anything at all. Apart from fund-raising, which is important, collecting some data, and holding an occasional conference, the best thing the Democratic Party can do is get out of the way."

The Republican Advantage

Whether or not the Democratic Party has the will to promote women, it lacks the means. "The Republicans have a recruitment budget; we don't," says Don Foley, of the DSCC. The political consultant Ann Lewis explains that the Republicans also have an organizational advantage when it comes to promoting women. "The Republican Party is a top-down hierarchy with centralized fund-raising. The Democratic Party is best understood as a federation of state parties. The only truly national Democratic operation is the presidential selection process. Everything else is run state by state, and some states are surer, swifter, and richer than others."

Because they had more resources and more control over their own system, Republicans made more progress recruiting women

in the early 1980s, according to Lewis, who used to recruit for the
Democrats. "My Republican counterpart would go to candidates
and say, 'We'll get the nomination. We'll max on funding.' I'd say,
'Look, it's going to be a lot of fun, but you're going to have to fight
for the nomination, and maybe I can get you a dollar.'"

Republicans also had more incentive to recruit women candidates after the gender gap appeared, in 1980, showing that wom-
en were more likely to vote Democratic. According to Kathy Wilson, a board member of the National Republican Coalition for
Choice, "The gender gap scared them to death. The appointment
of Sandra Day O'Connor was no accident. Republicans are
shrewd, and they realize they need women to temper the Republican image." Republicans, because "they are better marketers than
Democrats," are interested in fielding women, Ann Lewis says,
summing things up. "Democrats think of politics as organizing.
Republicans think of politics as marketing."

But Republicans have had the same problem marketing wom-
en candidates that Democrats might have had marketing Strate-
gic Defense Initiative [SDI]. The party has a credibility problem
on women's issues. Running as a Republican can be a disadvantage to women candidates who seek support from women voters
concerned with such issues as abortion, family leave, and health
care. Claudine Schneider, a former congresswoman from Rhode
Island who unsuccessfully challenged the incumbent senator
Claiborne Pell in 1990, is convinced that she would have fared
better as a Democrat. "Many women believe the myth that Republicans are bad for women and Democrats are good for them," she
says. Lynn Martin, who lost a 1990 Senate race in Illinois to the
incumbent Democrat Paul Simon, reports a similar disadvantage
among women voters: "One group of voters won't vote for you
because you're a woman; another group of women voters won't
vote for you because you're a Republican." (Martin does not attribute her loss to bias; like Claudine Schneider, she was up against a
popular incumbent.)

"The Republican Party is interested in the concept of promoting women, but they have an ideology problem," Ann Lewis says.
During the 1980s the party's primary electorate became increasingly conservative—anti-abortion and strongly in favor of "traditional" family roles—and resistant to electing women. Democrats
have no similar ideology problem, but they have financial and
organizational problems and, it seems, lack the requisite marketing skills—the ability to dramatize their message.

The Difficulty of Telling Their Own Stories

A campaign is a morality play, in the view of Larry K. Smith, a former manager of a presidential and several senatorial campaigns, and now counselor to the House Armed Services Committee. "A campaign is a contest over values and norms, not issues," he says. "Every campaign is a story about the candidate and the nation." The Democratic Party has distanced itself from voters, Smith suggests, by taking a "literalist" approach to campaigning, rather than a dramatic one. Instead of telling a first-person story about values, it has told a third-person story about issues.

Whether this is an accurate assessment of the Democratic Party in general (and not just of the 1988 Dukakis campaign), it does provide a useful perspective on women in politics. Women candidates have stories to tell different from men's, because, like it or not, they represent to voters different visions of authority and different values.

The primary storytellers in campaigns, however, aren't candidates but their media consultants—the majority of whom are men. They tend to imagine campaigns in ways that are inapposite to many women: their favorite campaign metaphors involve football and war; they tend to see themselves as hired guns. The consultant Wendy Sherman, a partner in the Washington firm Doak, Shrum, Harris, Sherman, Donilon and one of few women at the top of her field, suggests that the failures of male consultants to women are failures of imagination: "Consultants often get caught up in what is conventionally wise, and generally what's conventionally wise is what white men believe—because there are more of them inside the Beltway in positions of power."

That men's conventional wisdom sometimes misconceives women's political potential was demonstrated by Barbara Mikulski's successful 1986 Senate campaign. She was a popular congresswoman seeking an open seat in a contested primary, but "people inside the Beltway said she could not become a senator," Sherman, who was Mikulski's campaign manager in 1986, told me. "She didn't look like a senator, she didn't act like a senator, she didn't sound like a senator." For voters, however, that turned out to be the essence of her appeal. Sherman explained, "They looked at her and said, 'She's ours, and we may finally have a voice in the U.S. Senate, and we don't look like senators either.'"

The connection voters felt to Mikulski partly reflected her history of service in the House, Sherman added, but it also reflected and was strengthened by her sex. That women candidates seem more accessible to voters is indeed part of the new conventional wisdom; it's evidenced by the tendency to call women in authority by their first names.

Because women are expected to be more nurturant than men, one of the biggest mistakes for a woman candidate, according to experts, is running harshly negative ads. A frequently cited horror story about a woman's campaign and a male consultant involves a series of negative ads that Bob Squier produced for Harriett Woods in her unsuccessful 1986 Senate campaign in Missouri—the "crying-farmer spots."

These were a series of interviews with a farmer and his wife suffering a foreclosure by an insurance company whose board included Woods's opponent, Kit Bond. Run as a dramatic three-part serial (like an AT&T commercial), the ad included a shot of the farmer breaking down and sobbing as he talked about losing his cows. It concluded with freeze frames of the farmer and Kit Bond, and attacked Bond for opposing a moratorium on farm foreclosures.

Wood and her staff initially opposed Squier's advice to air the spots early in the campaign. Then, against her better judgment, Woods says, she "caved in." She ran the ad, and it sparked a controversy that badly damaged her campaign. The local press was critical; the ad was deemed unfair and exploitative. Squier's partner, William Knapp, concedes that "the ad did not work as well as we would have liked," but believes that had Woods stayed on the attack, she would have prevailed. Instead, she fired Squier, her campaign seemed to be in trouble, and that became a story in itself. Woods believes that the image of an "inept" woman candidate who couldn't keep her own campaign in order resonated with voters and political elites.

Woods, now the president of the National Women's Political Caucus, does not believe that she lost the election simply because of the ad—"1986 was a year in which factory workers stayed home or voted Republican." She is no longer "brooding" about her loss, but in talking about Squier and the crying-farmer controversy, she stiffens with anger. Her mistake, she says, was not in firing Squier, as one spin on the story suggested; it was in hiring him. She was uneasy about his style and his understanding of her identity from the beginning: "I worried that he didn't care who I was; he could talk to me and never listen. So I arranged a lunch with him. I thought, If he knows who I am, I can trust him to translate it. We had the lunch, and he talked the whole time about himself."

Women's tales of male arrogance are legion in the political community, as they generally are in male-dominated occupations. You believe them or not, depending on your own experiences and sensitivities. The tales are hardly empirical evidence of bias, unconscious or intended. But they surely prove that women perceive bias and that they encounter difficulties in telling their own stories and forging their own political identities.

Despite the horror stories and the litany of complaints, however, prospects for women candidates seem to be dramatically improving. Women have impressive new fundraising networks, which enabled them to capitalize on outraged support for Anita Hill. Political outsiders are in vogue, and optimists expect women to gain at least fifteen to twenty seats in Congress this year [1992]. In the aftermath of the Thomas-Hill hearings, at the end of the Cold War, in the midst of a recession, with battles over abortion looming in the states, the new conventional wisdom from the women's political community is upbeat. (It will sound a little pat, but that's part of its appeal.) This is what you're likely to hear today from politically active women, and some men, pollsters, organizers, consultants, and candidates, Democrats and quite a few Republicans alike.

Feminine Stereotypes

Women are perceived as being more honest than men, so they benefit from general concern about corruption. Women are outsiders, so they benefit from the anti-incumbency mood (women embody change, everyone says). Women are perceived as being more compassionate than men and better at dealing with the quotidian domestic problems—day care, education, and potholes—that are displacing concern about communism and national defense (which men are considered better able to address).

Republicans and Democrats differ as to whether the current climate favors Republican or Democratic women. The pollster Celinda Lake says that the combined strengths of Democrats and women on domestic issues are helpful; Kathy Wilson, of the National Republican Coalition for Choice, says that the combination of Democratic and presumptively feminine values is hurtful: "Too much compassion makes people clutch at their wallets." Republican women, she says, offer both compassion and fiscal competence—a quality that is particularly important to women. Sometimes women's advantage on domestic issues is said to be offset by a lack of credibility on fiscal matters. But the presumption that women don't understand budgets is usually said to be balanced by the presumption that they're honest. The media consultant William Knapp says, "There's a sense that a woman may not know how to fill out a general ledger sheet, but at least she won't steal." Ann Lewis remarks, "The stereotypes that used to work against us are now working for us."

It is probably not realistic even to hope that women might someday win or lose elections without being helped or hurt by stereotypes. Campaigning is the art of the superficial: it's about rhetoric, not policy, the manipulation of images, not the exchange of ideas. And, as everyone I interviewed reminded me, voters have different images of men and women: Men are tougher, et cetera. Women care more about their constituents; they're better housekeepers—and, as Jane Addams once suggested, government is "enlarged housekeeping" on a grand scale.

The use of feminine stereotypes to advance a feminist agenda is a central, historic irony of the American women's movement. Late-nineteenth-century social reformers like Addams and Julia Ward Howe championed what were considered feminine virtues—honesty, compassion, and heightened concern for moral behavior—arguing that women, once empowered, would bestow good government and peace upon the public. Stereotypes of femininity helped to fuel the suffrage movement, providing a rationale for women's participation in political life. Many women sought the vote not for its own sake, as a matter of right, but as a means of achieving womanly reforms. Listening to women candidates today, you sometimes hear a similar argument for electing women to high office: with their different voices, women will foster cooperation instead of confrontation in domestic and foreign affairs; as nature's housekeepers, women will clean up the environment.

The dangers of using stereotypes like these should be clear to generations of women who have had to prove their unfeminine ability and had to fight for the right to exercise power overtly outside the home, as well as covertly within it. By claiming "feminine" virtues, women may effectively deprive themselves of "masculine" strengths. Whether women candidates can exploit feminine stereotypes without ultimately being defeated by them is an unasked question at the heart of many women's campaigns.

Women politicians can hardly avoid stressing the qualities attributed to them which voters find appealing, but they have to stress them carefully, in very particular ways. "If a woman runs for governor and says, 'I'm gentler, nicer, and like children better,' she sounds as if she's running for day-care supervisor," Ann Lewis remarks. "On the other hand, what she can say is 'I know what real life is like. I know what budgets are like, what it is like to pay hospital bills and try to make ends meet. And when I go to the governor's office, I'll bring that knowledge with me.'"

Voters of both parties are likely to be persuaded by this message, Celinda Lake suggests, particularly during a recession; she observes in a 1991 report, "Winning With Women," that voters believe that women are better at "meeting the needs of the middle class." Lake surveyed about 1,160 voters, testing their reactions to "generic" male and female Republican and Democratic candidates. (She found, for example, that a generic Democratic woman would fare better than a generic Democratic man against a generic Republican man.) The trouble with this study, of course, is that neither campaigns nor candidates are generic; if all politics is local, then every race is unique, as is every candidate.

Some women also point out that previous predictions of victories for women did not come true. They said that women would win in 1990, the Republican pollster Linda DiVall recalls, but eight women ran for the Senate and seven lost. Claudine Schneider, who lost her 1990 challenge to Claiborne Pell, says that "for the first time," women's political future seems "foggy." Schneider says, "I still believed that with eight women running for Senate in 1990, at least half would be elected. When I lost, I was disappointed. When all the other women lost [except for the incumbent Nancy Kassebaum], I was devastated."

Congresswoman Pat Schroeder, too, is less than hopeful. She says, "The same women have been talking optimism for a long time, but here we are, in 1992, and we have only twenty-eight women in the House." Schroeder is also skeptical about assessments of the national mood and people's preoccupation with domestic concerns. "Something like the Gulf War rolls around, and the mood changes overnight. You could change the polls in two days if you suddenly got everyone in their flight suits bombing Qaddafi. The testosterone is flowing, and everyone's cheering—guys in the reserves put on their suits and they run the military hardware in the mall and crawl all over it. Great images."

At the national level, Schroeder adds, the electorate's focus shifts back and forth between domestic and international issues, and men are considered better able to handle both. In other words, men are less disadvantaged by stereotypes on domestic issues than women are on foreign policy. Schroeder says, "We'd look sillier than Dukakis in a tank."

Traditional images of women pose the stubbornest challenge on national-security issues. The challenge comes from voters who don't trust women's capacity for military command and also from within the feminist community. There is a strong, historical strain of pacifism in the women's movement, embodied by Jeannette Rankin, the first woman elected to Congress. Rankin voted against the popular resolution to declare war against Germany in 1917, to the dismay of her constituents. She voted her conscience and lost her office; she was defeated in a race for Senate the following year. She never recanted her vote or her pacifism. Fifty years later she was marching to protest the Vietnam War. Rankin died in 1978, at ninety-two, having devoted much of her life to the peace movement. She is an American feminist hero; at women's rallies against the Gulf War last year, her name was invoked, along with the image of women as peacemakers.

Jeannette Rankin is, however, a problematic role model for women candidates. Not every woman will or should sacrifice her office for a symbolic vote of conscience. Not every woman will or should be a pacifist; and to advance in the Senate and into the White House, women will have to convince the voters that they're prepared to go to war.

That may seem self-evident, but within the women's community it is a highly controversial position, an unholy assertion of feminist machismo. "We would know we had the first woman candidate for President when we saw a woman senator on a battleship, reviewing the troops," Ann Lewis recalls saying to a group of women. "And someone said, 'That's terrible. Do we have to repeat the military tradition?' And I said, 'No, you don't have to repeat it. You can vote for Mother Teresa.'"

This dialogue between pragmatism and purity is a staple of the women's community. In the Rankin tradition, significant factions of women have long practiced a politics of purity, promising to reform and cleanse the world in their own image, holding women candidates to higher standards than men, and seeking, in Lewis's words, "higher visions of ourselves."

The persistence and pervasiveness of this tradition and its broad implications for electoral politics are difficult to measure. Women candidates do commonly complain, however, that they are held to higher standards by voters than men are. The political double standard, like the double standard of sexual behavior, reflects both negative and positive stereotypes of women: voters tend to have lower expectations of women's ability and higher expectations of their intent. The suspicion that women are less competent than men gives them less leeway to make mistakes. The notion that women are more moral than men makes them more accountable for behavior that raises even minor moral questions.

In addition, women's funding networks are said by candidates and campaign managers to be tougher on their candidates than men's networks, according to a 1989 survey by Celinda Lake. And women candidates may have unrealistic expectations of their constituents, Lake suggests today. "I don't think women's interest groups are tougher; I think women candidates expect them to be easier. Running for office is a very isolating experience for a woman. Candidates want to believe they can go back to women supporters for nurturance."

In fact in recent years the women's political community has become more "tough-minded" than nurturant. In Washington, at least, pragmatism has clearly displaced purity. Organizations like EMILY's List, a Democratic fund-raising network, the National Women's Political Caucus, and the Women's Campaign Fund practice savvy, bottom-line politics, supporting only those candidates deemed to be electable. This practice is not universally acclaimed, however. Patricia Ireland, the president of the National Organization for Women, dismisses it as a "politics of scarcity" that deters qualified women from running. She prefers "flooding the ticket."

While organizations like EMILY's List and the National Women's Political Caucus represent the new insider politics for women, NOW remains on the outside, along with Ellie Smeal's Fund for the Feminist Majority. Insider women—lobbyists and consultants—often deride NOW for obstructionist ideological purity, pointing out that politics is the art of the possible; but that may not be quite fair. Activists like Ireland and Smeal view the possibilities differently. "I think we're the ones who are pragmatic," Smeal remarks.

A Women's Party?

Patricia Ireland and Ellie Smeal advocate the formation of a third party, not just for women but, as Ireland says, "for all people excluded from power"—a rainbow coalition of the marginal. It's hardly surprising that insider feminist women prefer to put their faith in the Democratic Party, rejecting this idea, sometimes gently and sometimes with contempt. Lynn Cutler, the vice-chair of the Democratic National Committee, calls creating a third party "the most self-destructive endeavor for women I can imagine." Pat Schroeder suggests that it's premature to talk about a third party, because "we don't yet have a second party."

Smeal isn't interested in reforming the Democratic Party, because of her firm belief that "the Republican boys and Democratic boys have more in common with each other than they do with a feminist agenda." The Democratic girls and Republican girls, she adds, have more in common with each other as well. Smeal puts her faith in sexual solidarity.

It's highly likely that since the Thomas-Hill hearings more women of both parties have sympathized with Smeal's position than had before. Linda DiVall speculates that "as a long shot," women may cross party lines in November [1992] to vote for one another. Jane Danowitz, of the Women's Campaign Fund, suggests that the hearings have lessened party loyalties for Democrats particularly and have diminished the importance of ideology in campaigns: "Before the hearings, issues like reproductive choice were paramount over gender, and there was a feeling that good men were as good as good women. But those good men failed us. We'll come of age when we realize that a mediocre woman is as good as a good man."

Smeal says she learned this lesson and came of age more than a decade ago, when she unsuccessfully lobbied the Illinois legislature to pass the Equal Rights Amendment. "We were dressed in green and the STOP-ERA women were dressed in red. We were the cheerleaders and the guys were on the field, strutting around and guffawing at their stupid sexist jokes. I woke up and saw that this was a stag game and even the good guys play it."

Smeal recalls a male United Auto Workers lobbyist explaining to her, "It doesn't matter if they're Democratic or Republican. It doesn't matter if they're liberal or conservative. It doesn't matter if they're pro-labor or anti-labor. What matters to them is that there's a card game in the back room and you women don't know where it is. Democrats, Republicans, liberals, and conservatives are all playing cards back there. They're afraid if they let you in, you're going to find their card game and you'll say, 'You shouldn't be back here playing cards; you should be out there working,' because that's what wives and mothers always do."

Ellie Smeal's bleak image of sexual politics is powerfully depressing. (And I don't ever want her mad at me.) She articulates some of women's worst fears about male bonding, while the hope she offers of female bonding seems less compelling.

Smeal is convinced that once there are enough women in any legislature to form a critical mass, they will vote in the interests of their sex. (Accept for the sake of argument the questionable underlying assumption that those interests are clear.) She suggests, for example, that a moderate Republican, such as Nancy Kassebaum, would be more likely to promote a feminist agenda if she were one of thirty women in the Senate rather than one of just two. Kassebaum doesn't agree. "Women don't march in lockstep, nor should they," she asserts. "It diminishes women to say that we have one voice and everything in the Senate would change if we were there."

Each point of view has considerable support among political women. "If we had fifty percent women in Congress instead of five percent, we'd have family and medical leave," Patricia Ireland declares. "I don't want women there for the sake of diversity; I want them there because I think our issues would move faster." Madeleine Kunin, the former governor of Vermont, says she saw changes in the voting patterns of the Vermont legislature as women gained more seats. But Lynn Martin says, "You belong to your party. You don't just vote by sex. The ballot says Lynn Martin (Rep.), not Lynn Martin (Fem.)."

The debate about the importance of sex is constant. Are you a woman candidate or a candidate who happens to be a woman or both? And how does sex interact with race or ethnicity in party politics? Carol Moseley Braun, the Democratic African-American who successfully challenged Alan Dixon in Illinois this year, says that she will "play the gender card" in a campaign, indicating to women voters that she offers them a voice on their issues, but that she will not "play the race card," making a similar appeal to the black community. "Race is too divisive," she explains.

Why is an appeal to sexual solidarity not divisive too? Perhaps because sexual loyalties have always been mitigated by race (and class) more than race has been mitigated by sex.

Do party loyalties also trump sex? It is axiomatic within the feminist community that if there had been more women in the Senate, the Thomas nomination would have been doomed. But half of the (two) women in the Senate voted to confirm him, and several Republican women who ran for the Senate in 1990 say they would have confirmed him too.

Probing the remarks of women from both parties, however,

you find that there is more agreement about the importance of sex than first appears. Republicans who stress that women vary ideologically (usually meaning that not all women are feminists) also stress that women have perspectives different from men's, which reflect their different life experiences and maybe even something in their nature. Republican and Democratic women often say that they would devote more attention than men to issues involving children and family life, regardless of how they would vote to address those issues.

There is, finally, some empirical evidence that women legislators do have perspectives different from men's, which lead to different legislative results. According to *The Impact of Women in Public Office*, a study released by the Center for the American Woman and Politics [CAWP], at Rutgers University, women are making a "profound and distinctive" difference in their legislatures, promoting popular feminist concerns: "Elected women are working to make the agendas of legislative institutions more responsive to women's demands for equal rights as articulated by the contemporary women's movement and more reflective of women's concerns stemming from their roles as caregivers in the family and in society." Based on telephone interviews with male and female state legislators, the CAWP study asserts that men and women tend to have different policy priorities. Women, it says, "were more likely to give top priority to women's rights policies" and to "policies dealing with children and families and health care."

The Gender Gap

It should go without saying, but probably doesn't, that regardless of how women would vote in the Senate, they have a right to be there. Women candidates should not have to earn access to the Senate as they once "earned" the right to vote, by promising to make the world a kinder, gentler place. Still, as a practical matter, candidates have to satisfy the expectations of their constituents. How does the electorate divide on women's issues and the need for more women in office?

Candidates often say that polling data indicate that equally small numbers of voters would or would not vote for a woman on account of her sex. The majority of voters say that they consider the issues. It's difficult to know, however, how these statements correspond to behavior. Many people probably wouldn't say that they vote on the basis of sex, and many people are probably affected by unconscious biases. Celinda Lake and several candidates report that the strongest support for women candidates comes from educated, professional women under forty-five; the strongest opposition comes from older women who have fulfilled traditional domestic roles. There seems to be little if any hard data about the accuracy of these generalizations as applied to different racial and ethnic groups.

Everybody knows there's a gender gap—differences in male and female voting patterns—but nobody knows how wide it is or how deep or reliable. As Eleanor Holmes Norton, the nonvoting delegate to the House from the District of Columbia, says, "We've been hearing about it, seeing evidence of it, for at least twelve years, and yet have been blown away by anti-feminist men. At some point we ought to stop talking about the gender gap and try to understand it."

So what precisely do we know about the gender gap? According to Virginia Sapiro, a professor of political science at the University of Wisconsin, we know this: more women than men vote Democratic. We might also say, however, that more men than women vote Republican; and in fact, Sapiro says, the gender gap was caused by men leaving the Democratic Party while women stayed put. She adds, "When the discussion about the gender gap began, the question was 'What is it about women?'— reflecting an unspoken assumption that women are fickle. The question should have been 'What is it about men?'" Sapiro suspects that men became more conservative during the Reagan years partly in reaction to "the wimpiness of the Carter years," as typified by the hostage crisis. But, she cautions, this, too, is merely speculation.

So there is a partisan gender gap, for some reason or other, and since women register to vote in greater numbers than men, it can be said to favor the Democrats. But, as Linda DiVall says, the gap can be bridged: Republican men, for example, can sometimes win women's votes by attaching themselves to issues such as health care and Social Security.

We know that there is also a gender gap on issues, as DiVall's strategy implies. Women are less likely to favor cutoffs in social spending, Virginia Sapiro says, and they're less likely to favor war.

The gender gap on issues is changeable, however, as Sapiro stresses. She says, "The gap on social-welfare issues will lessen if men start losing faith in the economic policies of the last ten years." And the gender gap on issues is much more complicated than it first appears. For example, it is conventional wisdom that concern about the economy helps women candidates, but the truth of that hope, or fear, depends on how people analyze the economic crisis. Sapiro explains, "Everyone agrees the economy is a problem. Some will blame it on policies that favored the rich at the expense of the poor, and will talk about homelessness and the need to improve social services. Some will blame it on the deficit and the fact that we've been too wimpy with the Japanese. People aren't going to vote for women to stand up to the Japanese."

"Now, that's gender politics, that's a gender gap," Sapiro concludes. "But it's a lot more complicated, unpredictable, and interesting than the gender gap is usually supposed to be."

"There are a lot of pieces on this chessboard," Eleanor Holmes Norton remarks. The gender gap is also complicated by racial and class issues. It cuts across racial lines, Norton believes, but with varying degrees of incisiveness. Take women's reactions to the Thomas-Hill hearings: sex interacted with race and class to divide public opinion every which way. Nonprofessional women seem to have found Anita Hill hard to believe, because they saw her as a woman with choices. Black women, Norton observes, were particularly troubled by the fact that Hill's allegations were made "at the last minute," because of a traditional concern within their community for procedural fairness, reflecting a history of unfair trials. "Blacks are very procedurally sensitive."

Still, many political women speculate hopefully that the Thomas-Hill hearings have activated diverse groups of women voters. Combined with fury over reversals of abortion rights, anger at the Thomas-Hill hearings may prove to have considerable political potency.

Or then again, it may not. When I spoke with her, Pat Schroeder was not sanguine. "I think women are feeling politically homeless more than empowered," she said. "You've got to win some now and again." Women in the House had just lost a battle on family leave [1992], and Schroeder was contemplating powerlessness, including her own, and women's difficulties in confronting it. "Congresswomen aren't powerful. You get to the cloakroom and you're supposed to play ball. Women's issues aren't considered important. You're supposed to put them aside, not embarrass your colleagues, get with the program. 'Why don't you get on with something that matters?' they say. 'Why do you keep nagging us about family leave? And when you protest caps on sex discrimination in the Civil Rights Bill, they say, 'Aren't you petty?'"

Most women do not want to hear this from her, Schroeder says. "It sounds too painfully familiar. Most women feel in their core so much more vulnerable than men. They don't want to hear from a Pat Schroeder that congresswomen don't get powerful."

Schroeder is probably voicing what many political women feel, at least on occasion—as do some men, for individual congressmen probably don't have much power either. Balancing Schroeder's pessimism with the official optimism of the professional political women's community, you may glean some sense of how much and how little women progress. Despite the proliferation of focus groups and polls, assessing women's political prospects is hardly a science, and the best predictions are often confounded by irrational, uncontrollable events. You can characterize the American public as fundamentally decent and fair, or you can characterize it as fundamentally biased, ignorant, and cruel. Sometimes both characterizations seem equally true.

A lot of Americans are ready to elect more women to national and statewide office. And, as Pat Schroeder says, "A lot of Americans believe that Elvis is alive." Schroeder has been listening to talk radio, which is "vehemently anti-woman." She says, "I think they've decided to attack women with incredible vengeance because they're not afraid of us. They don't think we'll come and shoot them. Listen to hate radio for a week. Women who hope to break into the Senate had better be ready for trouble."

THE YEAR OF THE SEXIST WOMAN[2]

At last, it looks as though it's really going to be the Year of the Woman. Four women are predicted to secure seats in the Senate; 20 in the House. But this may not be the most significant change. This Year has also ushered in a different campaign style for female candidates. Many have been packaged in a decidedly unfeminist way. Namely, as Women.

Their strategists and consultants call this refreshing. Women

[2]Article by Karen Lehrman. From the *Wall Street Journal* A10:3O 12 '92. Reprinted with permission.

don't have to run away from their gender anymore. More important, this strategy better exploits the factors that make this election so amenable to women—anti-incumbent fever, the Hill-Thomas fiasco, the end of the Cold War, the near-end of *Roe v. Wade*: The important thing right now is to win.

Well, yes. But it's unclear how many votes women would be losing if they ran as individuals who happen to be women, signifying change nonetheless. Regardless, this gender-first strategy may not be simply a one-election phenomenon. And, as is the case with any form of sexism, it has coughed up numerous paradoxes (for one, it's being used by Democrats much more than Republicans). Most disturbing, it's not too hard to see how it could be turned against women at any time.

The Four Truths in 1992

The strategy seems to hold four truths to be self-evident:
• *Biology is destiny.* An implicit theme of this Year has been: Vote for me because Congress needs more women. Men who are good on "women's issues" aren't good enough; only a woman will do. "We'll come of age when we realize that a mediocre woman is as good as a good man," says Jane Danowitz of the Women's Campaign Fund, the oldest bipartisan PAC for women. The corollary to this is: If you don't vote for a woman, you must be sexist. Democratic strategists in Pennsylvania are already blaming Lynn Yeakel's possible loss on men who won't vote for women. What this analysis ignores is that there may be men—and women—who find Ms. Yeakel's qualifications meager and her knowledge of issues thin. (She did tell the Washington Post, "If they want to balance the budget, then balance it!")

Political affirmative action, which previously turned up in Bella Abzug's plan for Democrats to *nominate* only women, also makes the qualifications of the other women candidates moot. Moreover, an unqualified woman can only reinforce the politics-is-a-male-thing attitude that still pervades Capitol Hill.

The heady excitement of this Year has also created an atmosphere where mere public criticism of a woman is considered sexist or a betrayal of the larger cause. Patty Murray, the mom in tennis shoes running for the Senate in Washington state, reportedly equates criticism of her qualifications with male condescension toward women. In New York, Elizabeth Holtzman was skewered by the feminist establishment for daring to engage in (fairly

legitimate) negative advertising against Geraldine Ferraro, most
likely costing her the Democratic Senate primary to Robert
Abrams [1992]. Not only is Ms. Holtzman—as a woman—not
supposed to say nasty things (see below), but she's especially not
supposed to say them about a sister.

• *All women think alike.* The Year of the Woman hasn't cele-
brated just any woman, only women who toe a certain (liberal)
political line.

That would be fine, if it were stated flat out. But instead there
is talk of wanting to elect more Women as though they are all of
the same political bent. According to polls, women do tend to see
a slightly greater role for government in domestic affairs than do
men and a lesser role for the military. But that hardly translates
into a "woman's point of view." Establishment feminists have long
presumed to speak for women on subjects that have little relation
to equality for women. (The National Organization for Women's
new 21st Century Party definitively ties feminism to a wide-
ranging political agenda.) Female candidates should say they represent no one's "voice" but their own.

• *All women are born with certain inalienable traits.* One of the
more explicit parts of the strategy has been: Vote for a woman
because women are more honest, compassionate, selfless, emotional, pacific, conciliatory, caring, moral. This is based on extensive polling, on the long-held feminist presumption that women
would make politics more respectable (some suffragettes used
this argument to help win the vote), and on the "essentialist"
writings of feminist academics (Marilyn Quayle's "essential nature" speech at the GOP Convention was terribly PC).

Of course, these are all wonderful qualities. The problem is in
making them the special province of one gender. Wouldn't that
mean, then, that there might be other traits—say, strength, resolve, rationality, logic—that are not particularly common to
women? These traits are usually considered important for presidents. By cultivating old stereotypes, could women be creating
their own political glass ceiling? How will these innately pacific
women be able to defend a woman's right to serve in combat, let
alone lead the country into war? Moreover, if women are so naturally maternal—I can hear the hard right strategizing—why not
send them back to the home, where so many troubles today lie?

Meanwhile, the candidates themselves have not exactly lived
up to their ideal. Take the claim that women are more virtuous.
Democratic Rep. Mary Rose Oakar of Ohio ranks as one of the

top 22 abusers of checking privileges, with 213 overdrafts at the
House Bank. Ms. Yeakel paid more than $17,000 in back city
taxes a day before announcing her candidacy. If these women
don't fulfill their presumed destiny of changing "the nature of
power," would that mean women don't have much to offer the
public sector?

• *Women are better at homey domestic concerns.* Because of their
superior hormones and the experiences they've had raising children and caring for aging parents, the fairer sex is purportedly
better able to deal with the country's health, education and welfare.

Since "women have to manage the household, we can do better with managing this nation's finances," Illinois Democratic
Senate candidate Carol Moseley Braun told "Face the Nation."
Says Patty Murray: "As a woman going to work, I know how
important it is that we have good transportation so I can get my
kids to day care, run to my job, get to the grocery store, get
somebody else to baseball and get home in time." Democratic
consultants recommend that the women candidates use ads that
highlight such activities as trips to the mall.

It's time, the argument goes, for the tasks women do on a
daily basis to be considered top-notch experience for political
office. Women are finally challenging the image of who is fit to
govern, instead of trying futilely to conform to a very masculine
one. And, again, you can't be seen as part of the wheeling and
dealing if you portray yourself as primarily a homemaker (even
when you've been involved in politics for years).

Housework and Men's Work

Certainly breaking the millionaire-white-male-politician mold
is long overdue, and child rearing and housework shouldn't be
denigrated. But these experiences can't supersede political competence. And exploiting them just perpetuates the perception
that only women can perform these tasks, that they are "women's
experiences."

A survey by the Center for the American Woman and Politics
found that women state legislators do tend to give more priority
to issues relating to the family. But there's a big difference between making an issue a priority (which has much to do with the
fact that men have regrettably never done so) and being able to
solve the problem. Saying only women can deal with these issues

not only continues to ghettoize them, it reinforces another old stereotype: that women can think only about problems they've directly experienced. And, again, if women are naturally better at domestic policy, does that mean they're naturally not so good at foreign policy?

The alternative to exploiting gender is not "imitating men." Women should run for office on their merits, as individuals. With any luck, as the number of women lawmakers grows, the concept of some single-minded sisterhood will lose its validity. Seems that might have been the whole point of feminism.

THE YEAR OF THE WOMEN[3]

For a moment there, it looked as if they had Bob Dornan. Less than two weeks before the primary, the California Republican's own polling figures showed challenger Judith Ryan moving within 10 points—with a whopping 27 percent of the district still undecided. Feminist leaders made the outspoken Congressman Dornan their Willie Horton, and a consortium of abortion-rights, gay, and otherwise Democratic outfits poured somewhere between $300,000 and $600,000 into the primary race.

They were abetted by a willing press. The *New York Times, Wall Street Journal, Los Angeles Times,* National Public Radio, and others all contributed stories on Dornan's vulnerability; one of them, by the *Washington Post*'s Judy Mann, even became a Ryan campaign handout. Kate Michelman of the National Abortion Rights Action League and Patricia Ireland of the National Organization for Women flew out to California for a victory celebration primary evening. *Good Morning America* even booked Judge Ryan for the show the next morning for a nationally televised wake.

But they turned up short one corpse.

When the final tally came in, Dornan had won by a 60 to 40 landslide. Nor was he the only one to stump the conventional wisdom. In another closely watched race, Joan Milke Flores defeated Maureen Reagan, and a crop of other conservative and

[3]Article by William McGurn. From *National Review* 44:21–22 Jl 6 '92. Copyright © 1992 by National Review, Inc. Reprinted with permission.

pro-life Republican women—Donna Peterson in Texas, Pam
Roach in Washington, Linda Bean in Maine—is breaking the stereotype of women politicians as Pat Schroeder clones. So you will
not find them getting money from groups like EMILY's List (Early Money Is Like Yeast) or WISH (Women in the Senate and
House). What it all points to is that the women's movement has
more to do with ideology than with sisterhood.

"Where were these groups when Beverly Byron needed
them?" asks Dornan, referring to the Maryland Democrat who
just lost her primary. "She had an important seat on the Armed
Services Committee. But in her case they backed a pro-abortion
male over a pro-life female. So don't tell me that this is all about
getting women into Congress."

Dornan has a point. Ever since Carol Moseley Braun defeated
Senator Al Dixon in the Illinois Democratic primary and *60 Min-
utes* followed up with a puff-piece on EMILY's List, 1992 has been
touted as "The Year of the Women." When Lynn Yeakel won the
Democratic primary in Pennsylvania to challenge Senator Arlen
Specter (R.), the phrase was elevated from tag line to trend.

The idea is that American women intend to exact vengeance
for the treatment of Anita Hill by a male-dominated Capitol Hill.
Never mind that the *USA Today* and ABC News/*Washington Post*
polls all showed clearly that a majority of American women
thought Miss Hill was a lying you-know-what. What *American Spectator* editor R. Emmett Tyrrell calls the Kultursmog (Hollywood,
TV, the press) has swallowed it whole. The *Washington Post* just ran
a full-page ad about the episode of *Designing Women* dealing with
the characters' anger at the Thomas hearings. The June issue of
Life magazine sports a cover photo of the White House under the
headline, "If Women Ran America." And the current *Newsweek*'s
aptly named "Conventional Wisdom" has treated Barbara Boxer's
Democratic primary triumph in California as though it were the
election itself ("Anita Hill trumps rubber checks. See you in
Washington, Di Fi, Lynn Yeakel, and Carol Moseley Braun").

To be sure, there are more women candidates (186) for congressional office than usual. But what has the press all aflutter is
not women candidates but liberal Democratic women candidates.
As Bob Dole asked in a recent *Washington Post* op-ed, how many
stories have mentioned that since 1980 the Republicans have
nominated more women to run for the Senate than the Democrats have? In 1990 there were six Republican women running for
the Senate, but nobody called that "The Year of the Women."

And how come there were no Republican candidates present last week when the National Women's Political Caucus had its "Salute to the 1992 Women Candidates" on Capitol Hill?

Part of the reason has to do with the different ways Democratic and Republican women campaign. Republican women do not campaign on being women, they campaign as candidates with views on a host of issues. "We're kind of the outsiders' outsiders," says Donna Peterson, a graduate of West Point who is taking on Charlie Wilson in Texas's 2nd District. "We're outsiders because we're women, but we're also outsiders because we're outside the liberal agenda."

That agenda, moreover, is pretty narrowly defined. "It's abortion," says the Eagle Forum's Julie Hoffman. "If you're pro-life, none of the groups supposedly dedicated to getting more women into office will support you." Indeed, both EMILY's List (Democratic) and WISH (Republican) declare openly that only pro-choice women need apply. Women who fall outside this category have a harder time being heard than blacks who buck the civil-rights establishment.

On the Democratic side, this doesn't matter much in primaries, because with all the normal people having departed, the only ones left are the nuts. Thus it's not surprising that Democratic nominees enter their races spouting solidarity with Anita Hill and a commitment to abortion on demand. It's not even surprising that they rack up primary victories—though Miss Braun benefited from a third candidate, Al Hofeld, who spent millions of dollars on ads attacking Dixon.

Turnout was small, too, following the trend since 1972. "Democratic primaries are disproportionately dominated by women," says Democratic political writer Peter Brown, in his book *Minority Party*. "And the women that vote in Democratic primaries are not demographically representative of the electorate that will vote in November. So what you get is much the same situation that led people to nominate George McGovern in 1972."

When Dianne Feinstein captured the gubernatorial nomination in California two years ago, the papers had her setting up house in Sacramento as though Pete Wilson didn't exist. This year [1992], Lynn Yeakel, Barbara Boxer, and Carol Moseley Braun will also be facing opponents in November, and it's a tad early to start ordering furniture for their Senate offices. One might even wonder whether "The Year of the Women" signals less a resurgent feminist strength than the continuing Democratic anemia.

"What's going on in the Democratic Party is the siege of Leningrad," says Kate O'Beirne of the Heritage Foundation. "They've started sending women up to the front lines because they've run out of men."

DID AMERICA 'GET IT'?[4]

There they stand, two caryatids at the portals of 1992: Anita Hill, who ushered in the year, and Hillary Clinton, ushering it out on her way to the White House. Two women, both Yale-educated lawyers. One black and single, the other white and married. One a picture of powerlessness, trapped before a committee of uncomprehending men who just "didn't get it," the other a powerhouse First Lady-in-waiting—credentialed, outspoken and, up until now, a bigger breadwinner than her husband. In their way, Hill and Hillary—*the* woman of the year in this year of the woman— embody the debate about the political and social significance of 1992: when the ballots were tallied and the accomplishments ticked off, was the glass half empty or half full?

Pundits had confidently promised "The Year of the Woman" before this, only to find that the real political gains never quite matched the hopeful expectations of women's advocates. By most measures, however, 1992 has come closer to living up to the advance billing than '88 or '90 or even '72, when a Life Magazine cover story featuring Bella Abzug opened with the proviso "It may not quite be the year of the . . . " Four freshwomen will enter the Senate in January (half full), bringing the grand total up to six (half empty); 24 new women will join 23 veterans in the House (full), accounting for 11 percent of the votes (empty). Emily's List, the Democratic women's fund-raising group, fed approximately $6 million into House and Senate campaigns this year, making it the biggest congressional PAC—a clear victory in a process where nothing confers influence as much as money in the (very full) war chest.

[4]Article by Eloise Salholz with Lucille Beachy, Susan Miller, Peter Annin, Todd Barrett and Donna Foote. From *Newsweek* 120/26:20–22 D 28 '92. Copyright © 1992 by Newsweek, Inc. Reprinted with permission.

Judging the meaning of '92 merely in terms of winners and losers or dollars and cents, however, may ultimately be another way of not *getting it.* The fact is, women's issues dominated political discourse in a dramatic new way. The sexual assaults at Tailhook might have been dismissed as the peccadilloes of boys being boys, but—in the year of the woman—they instead triggered one of the worst scandals in naval history. Susan Faludi's "Backlash", a feminist call to arms, and Gloria Steinem's "Revolution From Within" rode the best-seller list. When Marilyn Quayle stood before the GOP convention, lecturing women about their "essential natures," she proved how out of touch the GOP was with the reality of their lives. Soon it was payback time: female voters, says "Megatrends for Women" author Patricia Aburdene, "elected Bill Clinton."

There are certain events whose historic significance emerges only bit by bit. Rosa Parks's refusal to give up her seat on the bus was one such seminal moment; the rioting at a Greenwich Village gay bar called Stonewall was another. Last fall's Judiciary Committee hearings transfixed the public; but given the nation's sound-bite attention span, it was by no means clear that Hill's testimony about Clarence Thomas would have such an extraordinary shelf life. Yet it not only has continued to matter, it is a still-evolving event: a *Newsweek* Poll last week found that 51 percent of the women surveyed now believe Thomas sexually harassed Hill, compared with only 27 percent in October '91. Carol Gilligan, a feminist psychologist at Harvard, believes the image of Hill and those men will define this age the way Nick Ut's searing photo of a napalmed child captured the Vietnam era.

If Hill's witness had come at another time, her legacy might have been confined to consciousness-raising—and '92 might have been just another year that wasn't. But the election season was moving into high gear, and women like Carol Moseley Braun in Illinois were quick to capitalize on the deep outrage over Hill's treatment. In an attempt to mine public disgust with politics as usual, some women made much of their outsider status. But while female candidates were able to seize the moment, many—notably Senator-elect Dianne Feinstein of California—had been toiling in local vineyards for decades. "These women did not jump full blown on the political stage," says Ruth Mandel, director of the Center for the American Woman and Politics at Rutgers. "This [was] a year when opportunity [met] preparedness, a well-deserved reward after 20 years of work."

The candidates weren't the only women making history: for
the first time, women voted the gender line. As recently as 1984,
women sent Geraldine Ferraro contributions and little notes saying, "I don't want my husband to know, but I'm supporting you."
Then, on Election Day, says Ferraro (who lost her bid for the U.S.
Senate this year), they "voted the same as men." But in the 1992
primaries, all the women winners except Feinstein owed their
victory to a disproportionate number of female votes. "Women
were gatekeepers," says political consultant Ethel Klein. "This
was an election where women said, 'We're going to respect
ourselves—and we're going to demand that you respect us'."

The message got across, partly because the terms of the debate had changed so drastically. In other elections, Democratic
presidential candidates had to prove they could push the button
as well as any Republican. Since the fall of communism, there was
no button. Instead, voters wanted to know what the candidates
were going to do about unbalanced budgets, education and
health insurance—"soft" issues often associated with women. So
1992 wasn't the year that the electorate abandoned stereotypes
about who was fit to handle the nation's problems. Instead, says
California pollster Mark DiCamillo, "gender stereotypes worked
to [women's] advantage." Patty Murray of Washington state ran
for the U.S. Senate as the "mom in tennis shoes," a slogan suggesting she knew all about schools, medical expenses and, of
course, supermarket scanners.

Arguably, the person who did the most to feminize political
rhetoric in '92 was Hillary's husband. Bill Clinton became the
Oprah of presidential politics, embracing not only women's issues
but womenspeak. "It became clear at the Democratic convention
that most of the good that had come to Clinton had come through
women, his mother and others," says poet Robert Bly, a founder
of the men's movement. "This is a man who got up there," adds
consultant Klein, "and told a personal story about putting himself
bodily in front of a raging stepfather who was about to hurt his
mother. That is at the core of the vulnerability women feel in this
society." Michael Dukakis, by contrast, supported many of the
same causes but couldn't connect emotionally—most notably
when asked a hypothetical question about his wife and rape. As a
result, he squandered the female franchise. Clinton, says sociologist Michael Kimmel, is "Anita Hill's revenge."

It is clear that women have had tremendous impact on the
political process this year; less clear is the impact of the political
changes on the lives of American women. Most of the respon-

dents in the *Newsweek* Poll believe women either made progress or held their ground in 1992; only 14 percent say women lost ground. While a majority of the women surveyed say that the men they know personally have become more sensitive to the needs and problems of women, 68 percent replied that most American men do not understand the issues that concern women most. Bill and Hillary Clinton may represent a generational shift from old-fashioned First Couple to postmodern partnership, but the sexes obviously find themselves still talking at cross-purposes.

Thanks to the confirmation hearings, there's far less static on the line when the subject is sexual harassment. "Every time a man and a woman meet at the water cooler now, Anita Hill [is] right there between them," says Andrea Sankar, an anthropologist at Wayne State University in Detroit. After the hearings, many firms reviewed existing sexual-harassment policies or implemented new ones. A survey in *Working Woman* magazine last June found that 81 percent of Fortune 500 companies offer sensitivity-training programs, up from 60 percent in 1988. According to the Equal Employment Opportunity Commission, where Hill and Thomas worked together, 10,522 people filed sexual-harassment complaints this year, compared with 6,883 in fiscal 1991. Following Maine's lead, Connecticut passed a law requiring that employers provide a harassment policy and sensitivity training for workers; similar statutes are pending in several other states.

Awareness about sexual harassment may be most acute at the scene of the crime. With allegations hanging over Senators Bob Packwood of Oregon and Daniel Inouye of Hawaii, legislators are tripping over each other to demonstrate their sensitivity—while quietly praying their own dirty little secrets don't come out. "Many senators are shaking in their boots because women are breaking the silence," says Gloria Allred, whose Los Angeles law firm handles many sexual-harassment cases. Since last winter, many senators—including Judiciary Committee members Arlen Specter, Alan Simpson and Joseph Biden—have attended consciousness-raising sessions led by the likes of Deborah Tannen, author of the best-selling *"You Just Don't Understand."* Taking no chances, Senator-elect Murray promises to introduce a bill making Congress accountable to the same sexual-harassment laws as everybody else.

Members of both sexes are waiting to see whether Washington's newest women will indeed bring a unique sensibility to the task of government. Clinton appointee Donna Shalala, who

served as an assistant secretary of HUD under Jimmy Carter,
noted that women looked at public housing differently than men.
"It's not just strategy," she told *Newsweek* before her appointment.
"It's that we know you don't [put in] showers when you have little
kids and need bathtubs." After an hourlong meeting, incoming
women representatives quickly settled on four priorities: fully
funding Head Start, passing family-leave legislation, codifying
legal abortion and rescinding Congress's immunity to sexual-
harassment laws. Will there be power in numbers? Colorado Rep.
Patricia Schroeder recalls her pioneer days in the early '70s, when
she found herself changing her children's diapers on the House
floor. Now carpenters are busily remodeling the Capitol to add a
ladies' room off the Senate floor. While they're at it, maybe they
should put in a changing table—and another, for good measure,
in the men's room. Now, that would be a sign of changing times.

BIBLIOGRAPHY

An asterisk (*) preceding a reference indicates an excerpt from the work has been reprinted in this book.

Books and Pamphlets

Astin, Helen S. & Carole Leland. Women of influence, women of vision: a cross-generational study of leaders and social change. Josey-Bass. '91.

Banner, Lois W. Women in modern America: a brief history (2nd ed). Harcourt Brace Jovanovich. '84.

Barciauskas, Rosemary Curran. Loving and working: reweaving women's public and private lives. Meyer-Stone Books. '89.

Batialle, Gretchen M., (ed). Native American women: a biographical dictionary. Garland. '93.

Berry, Mary Francis. The politics of parenthood: child care, women's rights and the myth of the good mother. Viking. '93.

Bravo, Ellen. The 9 to 5 guide to combating sexual harassment. Wiley. '92.

Campbell, Karlyn Kohrs. Man cannot speak for her. Greenwood Press. '89.

Chan, Anja Angelica. Women and sexual harassment: a guide to the legal protections of Title VII and the hostile environment claim. Haworth Press. '93.

Cohen, Marcia. The sisterhood: the true story of the women who changed the world. Simon and Schuster. '88.

Davis, Flora. Moving the mountain: The women's movement in America since 1960. Simon and Schuster. '91.

Eskenazi, Martin. Sexual harassment: know your rights. Carroll & Graf. '92.

Faludi, Susan. Backlash: the undeclared war against American women. Crown. '91.

Gordon, Suzanne. Prisoners of men's dreams: striking out for a new feminine future. Little Brown. '91.

Hine, Darlene Clark, (ed). Black women in America: an historical encyclopedia. Carlson. '93.

*Hochschild, Arlie with Anne Machung. The second shift: working parents and the revolution at home. Viking. '89.

Kahne, Hilda and Janet Z. Giele (eds). Women's work and women's lives: the continuing struggle worldwide. Westview Press. '92.

Lindemann, Barbara. Primer on sexual harassment. Bureau of National Affairs. '92.

Matthews, Glenna. The rise of public women: woman's power and woman's place in the United States 1630–1970. Oxford University Press. '92.

Mezey, Susan Gluck. In pursuit of equality: women, public policy, and the federal courts. St. Martin's Press. '92.

Michaels, Bonnie and Elizabeth McCarty. Solving the work/family puzzle. Business One Irwin. '92.

Moen, Phyllis. Women's two roles: a contemporary dilemma. Auburn. '92.

Morrison, Toni (ed.) Race-ing justice and en-gendering power: essays on Anita Hill, Clarence Thomas and the construction of social reality. Pantheon. '92.

Okin, Susan Moller. Justice, gender, and the family. Basic Books. '89.

Paludi, Michele Antoinette. Academic and workplace harassment: a resource manual. State University of New York Press. '91.

Petrocelli, William. Sexual harassment on the job. Nolo Press. '92.

Phelps, Timothy M., and Helen Winternitz. Capitol games: Clarence Thomas, Anita Hill, and the story of a supreme court nomination. Hyperion. '92.

Phillips, Anne. Engendering democracy. Pennsylvania State University Press. '91.

Posner, Judith. The feminine mistake: women, work and identity. Warner. '92.

Robertson, Nan. The girls in the balcony: women, men and the *New York Times*. Random House. 1992.

Schwartz, Felice N. Breaking with tradition: women and work, the new facts of life. Warner. 1992.

Seharan, Uma & Frederick, T. L. Leong. Womanpower: managing in times of demographic turbulence. Sage. 1992.

Shelton, Beth Anne. Women, men, and time: gender differences in paid work, housework, and leisure. Greenwood. '92.

Silberstein, Lisa R. Dual-career marriage: a system in transition. L. Erlbaum. '92.

Steinem, Gloria. Revolution from within: a book of self-esteem. Little Brown. '92.

Sumrall, Amber Coverdale & Dena Taylor (eds). Sexual harassment: women speak out. The Crossing Press. '92.

Swiss, Deborah J. & Judith P. Walker. Women and the work/family dilemma: how professional women are coping. Wiley. '93.

United States/Congress/House/Committee on Education and Labor/ Subcommittee on Employment Opportunities. Sexual harassment in non-traditional occupations. 102nd Congress. 2nd session. U.S. G.P.O. '92.

United States/Congress/House/Committee on Armed Services/Subcommittee on Military Personnel and Compensation. Gender discrimination in the military. 102nd Congress. 2nd session. U.S. G.P.O. '92.

United States/Congress/House/Committee on Armed Services. Women in the military: the Tailhook affair and the problem of sexual harassment. 102nd Congress. 2nd session. U.S. G.P.O. '92.

Wall, Edmund (ed). Sexual harassment: confrontations and decisions. Prometheus Books. '92.

Wood, Bette. Black women in the workplace: impacts of structural change in the economy. Greenwood. '92.

ADDITIONAL PERIODICAL ARTICLES WITH ABSTRACTS

For those who wish to read more widely on the subject of women's issues, this section contains abstracts of additional articles that bear on the topic. Readers who require a comprehensive list of materials are advised to consult the *Reader's Guide to Periodical Literature* and other Wilson indexes.

The real Anita Hill David Brock, *The American Spectator* 25:5 18–30 Mr '92

Judge Susan Hoerchner is the only person to emerge so far who made a connection between Anita Hill, Judge Clarence Thomas, and the charge of sexual harassment at the time of Thomas's nomination to the Supreme Court on July 1. A friend of Hill's, who later testified on her behalf before the Senate Judiciary Committee, Hoerchner told interviewers that she recalled a phone call in which Hill said she was being sexually harassed before September 1981. This period of time was, in fact, before Hill went to work for Thomas. Later, in a statement to the Senate, Hoerchner denied any knowledge of the date of the call. The writer describes evidence linking Hoerchner to sources in Washington, discusses reasons why Hill would make such a charge against Thomas, and chronicles the anti-Thomas movement's attempts to stop his confirmation. An editorial discusses reactions to the charges.

Dan Quayle was right Barbara Dafoe Whitehead, *The Atlantic* 271:47–50+ Ap '93

Contrary to the prevailing view, social-science evidence shows conclusively that the dissolution of intact 2-parent families is harming children. A growing body of research suggests that as more parents have divorced or had children out of wedlock over the past few decades, overall child well-being has declined. Problems of poverty, emotional dysfunction, educational failure, physical and sexual abuse, and unpreparedness for the future are all a part of this decline. Yet to insist that fragmented families are to blame provokes angry resistance. Cultural and ideological trends have helped spread the mistaken view that parents', and not children's, happiness is the most vital measure of familial success. Discussed are the recent history of family form and cultural norms, the media's impact, family law, the related social problems of crime and school decline, and the views of several family researchers. A sidebar examines public policies on the family.

The year of the black woman? Kitty Dumas, *Black Enterprise* 23:35 Ag '92

Black women are running for office in record numbers this year. Of the 150 women running for seats in the U.S. House of Representatives, close to 20 are African-American. In addition, there are now 4 women in the 26-member Congressional Black Caucus, and that number could grow this year. Sonia Jarvis, executive director of the National Coalition on Black Voter Participation, says that black women seeking office are often plagued by funding difficulties and rejection by male power brokers and sometimes by women voters. Still, many black women have decided to run. David Bositis of the Joint Center for Political and Economic Studies says that the explosion of female candidates was caused by the Voting Rights Act, which created more black districts; by the increase in women involved in local politics and by anger over the Senate's handling of the Clarence Thomas and Anita Hill case.

Corporate women *Business Week* 74–8+ Je 8 '92

A special section examines corporate women. There is a pervasive sense of inequality among U.S. women executives, judging by a recent Business Week survey of 400 female managers. Half of the women surveyed say that corporate America is doing somewhat better in terms of hiring and promoting women, but half also say that the rate of progress is slowing. The mood is more downcast than it was in a similar poll conducted in 1990. Now, 70 percent of those polled see the male-dominated corporate culture as hindering their success, 10 percent more than those who said so 2 years ago. Still, the 1990s might be a breakout decade if a combination of demographics and enlightenment, along with a little legal pressure, can coalesce. The top 50 women in business are listed, and profiles of Charlotte Beers of Ogilvy & Mather Worldwide, Jill Barad of Mattel, Linda Wachner of Warnaco, Michele Hooper of Baxter International, and Joan Lappin of Gramercy Capital Management are presented.

Getting serious about sexual harassment Troy Segal, *Business Week* 78+ N 9 '92

A growing number of companies are addressing the issue of sexual harassment, but there is still a long way to go. A year after the Anita Hill-Clarence Thomas hearings, the Equal Employment Opportunity Commission reports a 50 percent increase in harassment claims. Management consultants, labor lawyers, and private advocacy groups say that calls for information from companies and individuals have tripled. More than half the people polled in a recent National Association for Female Executives survey said that their companies have not addressed the problem. Those firms that do address the issue often rely on such token gestures as posting a policy or handing out a list of dos and don'ts. Companies need to reach beyond quick fixes to systematically educate and continue educating their work force.

Where are all the female B-school profs? Lori Bongiorno, *Business Week* 40 D 7 '92

Just 8 percent of tenured faculty at Business Week's Top 20 business schools are women, and several prominent business schools, including those at Dartmouth College and Washington University, have no tenured women. Diana R. Harrington, a professor at the University of Virginia's Darden School of Business, says that the system is controlled by a largely white, male club. Some business school deans, however, say that the supply of qualified women has long been limited and has only recently increased. Discussed are the cases of professor Melissa H. Burch, who charged discrimination after she was not recommended for tenure at the Darden School and who saw the decision reversed, and of professor Ceil M. Pillsbury, who was denied tenure at the business school at the University of Wisconsin at Milwaukee and whose dispute over alleged discrimination has not been resolved, although the Equal Employment Opportunity Commission urged that she be given tenure.

Mom is the boss *Ebony* 47:72+ S '92

A growing number of savvy career women have the ambition to achieve not only in the boardroom but also in the home. These well-educated, exceptionally talented women have determined that they want it all, and they are proving that they can excel in jobs that were once all-white and all-male and that they can be good mothers as well. Sylvia Rhone, chairwoman and chief executive officer of ATCO East-West Records; Sharon Smallwood Gund, senior vice president of Lockheed Information Management Services Co.; Amy Hilliard-Jones, director of market development for the baked goods division of the Pillsbury Co.; and Earlene Hardie Cox, director of taxes for IBM Credit Corp., are typical of this new breed. The ways in which these women maintain a balance between their careers and parenting responsibilities are discussed.

If you can't join 'em, beat 'em Nancy J. Perry, *Fortune* 126:58–9 S 21 '92

Part of a special section on women's progress in the workplace. Although women still face discrimination in the workplace, professional women should stop acting like victims and start beating men at their own game. A number of books and forecasts claim that women have fared badly in the workplace and that conditions are not improving. These claims, however, fail to take into account the tremendous progress that women have made in recent years. For example, the percentage of MBA degrees awarded to women rose from 25 percent in 1981 to 34 percent in 1990, the share of law degrees awarded to women jumped from 30 percent to 42 percent over the same period, and the median earnings of full time female workers increased by nearly 12 percent during the 1980s, while the average male's earnings dropped 6 percent. Advice for women hoping to get ahead in the workplace is provided.

I fought the system—and won Muriel Kraszewski, *Ladies' Home Journal* 109:24+ N '92

The writer describes how she won a sex-discrimination lawsuit against her former employer, State Farm Insurance Company. As a result of the suit, in which she charged that the company refused to hire her as an agent because she was a woman, State Farm was ordered to pay her more than $400,000. It also paid a total of $245 million to hundreds of other women who had been unfairly denied high-paying positions, the largest settlement ever awarded in a civil-rights case. A sidebar provides advice for those who believe that they have been the victim of gender discrimination.

A bitter brew Katherine Lanpher, *Ms.* 3:36–41 N/D '92

In 1991, 8 female employees filed a lawsuit against Stroh's Brewery, charging that Stroh's provided a sexually hostile work environment that was fostered by the company's advertising campaigns. The women have asked for more than $350,000 each in damages, and they have demanded that Stroh's stop sexually exploiting women in its advertising. The controversial lawsuit has pitted 2 feminist attorneys against each other—Lori Peterson, who represents the plaintiffs, and Carolyn Chalmers, who represents Stroh's. Peterson, who has frequently made provocative comments about the case to the media, argues that Stroh's ads have been used as a weapon of harassment and convey that sexism is acceptable. Chalmers contends that equating a beer poster with pornography is exaggeration and that incidents of sexual harassment at Stroh's were isolated. Only 1 of the 8 plaintiffs still works at Stroh's. A court date for the case is not expected to be set until 1993.

Striking a nerve *Newsweek* 118:34–8+ O 21 '91

Part of a special section on the issue of sexual harassment. For many
American women, sexual harassment is a fact of life. A Newsweek survey
showed that 21 percent of women polled had been harassed at work, and
42 percent said that they knew someone who had been harassed. Other
surveys indicate that more than 50 percent of working women have faced
sexual harassment at some point in their careers. Sexual harassment may
vary from a pattern of obscene joking to outright assault, and its emotional toll on victims is often profound and lasting. Over the last ten years, as
women have grown to represent nearly half the work force, the courts
have begun to act in cases involving sexual harassment. The Supreme
Court agreed in 1986 that sexual harassment is a violation of civil
rights. This decision and others have spurred hundreds of public and
private employers to write policies detailing appropriate behavior for employees.

Women scorned Katha Pollitt, *The Nation* 253:540–1 N 4 '91

The confirmation of Judge Clarence Thomas's nomination to the Supreme Court shows that the Democratic Party is neither willing nor able to
effectively oppose the ongoing right-wing revolution. When Professor
Anita Hill gave credible testimony that she had been subjected to sexual
harassment while working for Thomas, the Democrats seemed to forget
where they were and where their allegiances were supposed to lie. Clearly,
the men who come to power through the Democratic Party are never
going to bring the changing social relations between the sexes into the
political process in any real way. Women need to elect more feminists and
to refuse to vote for anyone who doesn't support the expansion of their
rights. In addition, they need to follow the lead of ACT representative
politics.

Stoop to conquer Ronni Sandroff, Abby Hirsch, *The Nation*
255:564–5 N 16 '92

This year's gubernatorial and congressional campaigns have provided ample evidence that while males are permitted to use aggressive campaign
tactics, female candidates are held to a higher standard. Several state races
are showing that women who avoid using negative campaign tactics are
still indirectly attacked by male opponents. These men criticize the wom-
en's friends and family members in an effort to hurt the female candidates themselves. The public professes to dislike negative ads, but such
ads are what the public always remembers. Female candidates must therefore be willing to fight back fiercely against male opponents, and their
supporters must also be willing to put up with such aggressive tactics. The
campaigns of Lynn Yeakel, Olympia Snowe, Carol Moseley Braun, and
Jennifer Dunn are discussed.

Womanifesto Jane O'Reilly, *The Nation* 255:77–8 Jl 20–27 '92

Part of a special issue on the political situation facing the Democratic Party. This election year is being hailed as the year of the woman because half the delegates to the Democratic National Convention are women, Texas governor Ann Richards is chairing the convention, and 7 promising female candidates are running for the Senate. This is really little more than hype, however. Women want much more from American politics: child care, family leave, health care, education, abortion rights, equal rights, an end to violence against women, a peace dividend, an end to scandals such as the S&L disaster, environmental protection, and above all, respect. The way to achieve these goals is to focus on electing as many women as possible to public office.

The parent trap Melinda Beck, *Newsweek* 121:34–7 F 1 '93

The child-care scandal involving attorney general nominee Zoe Baird highlighted the difficulties faced by working mothers. Thanks in part to the prevalence of illegal immigrants who are willing to work for low wages, more families at all income levels are paying illegal sitters to work in their homes. The writer discusses legal issues pertaining to domestic workers, attempts by domestic workers to combat exploitation, and legislation that may be supported by the Clinton administration to help working mothers. Sidebars present statistics about the child-care arrangements of working mothers in the United States and explain employers' obligation to pay social-security taxes for anyone who works around their homes.

The year of what woman? Susan J. Douglas, *The Progressive* 56:11 S '92

Despite talk of this being The Year of the Woman, mainstream media coverage of the recent Supreme Court decision on Planned Parenthood v. Casey showed that feminist and disadvantaged women are still being demonized and ignored. Touting the Court's ruling on the abortion case in favor of parental notification, a lecture by a doctor, and a 24-hour waiting period as the perfect abortion policy for all American women, the press legitimized a decision that imposes hardships and stress on less privileged and younger women while it labeled more progressive abortion opinions deviant and extreme. In reality, many Americans are uncertain about their views on abortion, and no ruling perfectly represents an American consensus. With the media screening out diversity of opinion on abortion, 1992 may become the year of the white, privileged woman rather than all women.

Hard times ahead for working mothers . . . but who cares? Elizabeth Ritchie Johnson, *Redbook* 176:89–90 Ap '91

Today's working mothers are having great difficulty juggling job and family responsibility. A mother who found that she was losing money by working recounts how she quit her job to free lance at home and talks about the need for reliable, affordable child care.

Anita Hill's legacy Jill Smolowe, *Time* 140:56–7 O 19 '92

Workplace sensitivity to sexual harassment has increased in the year since the confrontation between Anita Hill and Clarence Thomas, but women still fear pursuing harassment charges and face numerous obstacles when they do. The Equal Employment Opportunity Commission (EEOC) logged a record number of harassment complaints during the past year, indicating widespread awareness and a greater willingness on the part of harassment victims to take action. New books, television programs, academic courses, and corporate seminars have also boosted awareness. Nevertheless, many women still face difficulty in stopping workplace offenses, often afraid that they will be ignored, stigmatized, or fired when they report harassment to bosses who still consider such complaints insignificant. Even women who bring grievances to their companies or the EEOC encounter legal, financial, or bureaucratic difficulties that prevent them from resolving complaints.

What do women have to celebrate? Barbara Ehrenreich, *Time* 140:61–2 N 16 '92

Part of a special issue on the 1992 election. A record 117 women ran for seats in the House and Senate this year. Many people had previously declared feminism dead, but in 1992, Supreme Court restrictions on abortion rights and the Hill-Thomas hearings helped a generation of women voters realize that what they had taken for granted could be taken away. The female candidates had not only adrenaline but also achievements to build on; almost all of them had already served in a state legislature. What they needed for the big leap was money, and contributions began pouring in after the Hill-Thomas hearings. Moreover, many male legislators retired or declined to run again because of scandals, and other men were hurt by redistricting. The female candidates appealed not only to other women but also to men, who saw them as outsiders. The winners should not expect to accomplish too much, but whatever they do achieve will add to the credibility of the next wave of female candidates.

Harassment: men on trial Ted Gest, Amy Saltzman, *U.S. News & World Report* 111:38–40 O 21 '91

The problem of sexual harassment was scarcely acknowledged as a legal wrong until recent years, when women began entering the work force in large numbers. Surveys have found that about 40 percent of women contend that they have been sexually harassed at work, and a recent New York Times/CBS News poll reported that half of the men surveyed admitted to having done something that a woman might consider sexual harassment. The law now supports feminist arguments to broaden the definition of harassment, but few women have taken advantage of the change because they are either unaware of their rights or are afraid to exercise them. Moreover, federal law allows recovery only of lost wages and prohibits the punitive damages that other plaintiffs win to penalize companies.

The swearing never stops Gloria Borger, *U.S. News & World Report* 111:34–5+ O 28 '91

A special section examines the backlash over Anita Hill's accusations of sexual harassment against Supreme Court nominee Clarence Thomas. After Hill's charges became public, the fight escalated into a grueling, unfair, and manipulative drama with the intensity of a political campaign's last days. While Senate Judiciary Committee Democrats seemed intent on seeking the truth, Republicans pursued their singular goal of defending Thomas. Thomas's confirmation has sparked women's groups to charge Democrats with betrayal and Democrats to charge Republicans with dirty tactics. Republicans are now worried about alienating young women voters, and the Senate has vowed to change the confirmation process. Voters are disgusted with the whole process and have pledged to limit congressional terms. Articles discuss Thomas's stance on women's issues, the need to fix the culture of scandal in Washington, and the nationwide debate over sexual harassment.

A new interest in cracking the ceiling: women and minorities are getting a fairer shake Steven D. Kaye, *U.S. News & World Report* 113:80+ O 26 '92

Part of a guide to careers in the 1990s. In some companies, women and minorities are getting a fairer shake. For a variety of reasons, experts expect to see a new wave of companies—Lotus Development, Merck, Monsanto, and S. C. Johnson & Sons are among those on the leading edge—closely examining their promotion procedures. The move will be motivated in part by a sense of fair play and to some extent by arithmetic: Women and minority workers will represent 62 percent of the work force—and some 70 percent of the new entrants—by 2005. Fear is also driving the move, however. The 1991 Civil Rights Act gives female and disabled victims of discrimination the same right that minority victims have to sue for damages in addition to back pay. The article discusses mentoring programs at various companies.

Champions of child care Susan Seliger, *Working Mother* 14:54–6+ Je '91

A growing number of U.S. companies are recognizing that it is in their interest to offer their workers child care assistance. More than 5,000 companies now offer some form of child care help, up from little more

than 100 firms ten years ago, according to the Families and Work Institute
of New York. A recent survey of 463 firms showed that 74 percent expect
to offer child care resource and referral services by the year 2000, 35
percent say that they will set up on- or near-site centers, and 52 percent
say that they will probably subsidize child care expenses. The most common child care benefit options and some shining examples of each are
discussed.

Sexual harassment: the inside story Ronni Sandroff, *Working Woman* 17:47–51 Je '92

The response to Working Woman's survey on sexual harassment was over-
whelming. The survey revealed that almost 30 percent of harassment
incidents occur among women between the ages of 18 and 24 and that
harassment becomes much more common when women enter some predominantly male workplaces or breach the formerly all-male domain of
upper management. The article discusses the reasons why men harass
women in the workplace, what women should do if they are harassed, the
effects of harassment on women, and the odds of obtaining justice when
harassment is reported. Sidebars discuss the effect of the Anita Hill hearings on women voters and some of the steps that companies can take to
prevent sexual harassment.

Discrimination at the top Meryl Gordon, *Working Woman* 17:68–71+ S '92

An increasing number of women in top jobs on Wall Street, at law firms,
and in the rest of corporate America are realizing that even when they
reach the upper ranks, they lag behind male counterparts in pay, perks,
and power. According to the Equal Employment Opportunity Commission, the overall number of claims charging sex discrimination in promotion rose from 1,330 in 1986 to 2,083 in 1991. Many female high
achievers who have taken their employers to court for alleged sex discrimination seem stunned at what has happened to them. The recession has
complicated matters: As companies downsize, some women find themselves out of work, while their male colleagues are rotated to other departments or given generous severance packages. Many women who feel discriminated against in the upper ranks have been discriminated against
throughout their careers, but they realized it only later on. Several women
who have filed discrimination suits against their employers are profiled.

Being smart about the mommy track Barbara Kantrowitz, Pat Wingert, *Working Woman* 18:48–51+ F '93

Women who have tested the mommy track say that a work-schedule
change does not have to mean a loss of clout or credibility. Four years ago,
Catalyst founder Felice Schwartz suggested in an article that companies

think of female employees as either career primary women, who put work first, or career and family women, who, for a prolonged period, would need extra consideration from employers to balance their lives. She did not use the phrase mommy track, but that is the unflattering description that stuck for the second group. In the last 10 years, tens of thousands of women have altered their work schedules to accommodate their children. In most industries, professions, and jobs, it is proving possible to be an active mother and a valued employee. Moreover, some women are advancing their careers while raising children. Disadvantages of being on the mommy track are discussed, as are ways to advance a career while children are young and obstacles to avoid.